WALK WiTH A HUMBLE SWaGGER

MiCHaEL PaLMA

PRAISE FOR MICHAEL PALMA
AND *Walk with a Humble Swagger*

"For most people recruiting is a synonym for selling. The recruiter's job, in sports or business, is the act of convincing. Mike's not that kind of recruiter, probably because he was a much sought-after basketball recruit himself in his teens. Mike's not a seller, he's a teacher. His job is to give you the information and then let you make your own decision. He is authentic, honest, not a salesperson at all. I've known the guy for almost forty years now and he is full of many things. Information, stories, experience, life. One thing he is not full of, is shit. He's the real deal."

Steve Connelly Founder, Connelly Partners

"I've worked with Michael for more than 30 years. It's a relationship based on trust. Any time we have an important position to fill, there is only one person I would trust with the assignment. He gets our agency. He gets our business. And, because he's a competitive SOB he won't give up. I'm certain that comes from his time on the court."

Curtis Zimmerman Founder, The Zimmerman Agency

"GSD&M was just beginning to make a name for itself when a monotone voice on the other end of the phone introduced itself with *Hello, Guy, this is Mike Palma*. It was the first of more calls than I can count over the next several years, as Mike played an instrumental role in staffing my creative department, and GSD&M grew from a small regional shop into a national player—winning new business and awards in every significant competition along the way. Mike's ability to recognize and recruit top-caliber talent was a significant reason why. As a result, he not only became indispensable to me as an ECD, he became a trusted confidante and friend."

Guy Bommarito Executive Creative Director, GSD&M

"I first met Mike when he was a high school senior, almost forty-nine years ago. When I saw him again, I was a high school senior and visited Wake Forest where he was a player. Who knew that two years later we would be teammates and friends for over forty-six years. This book is a great read and I would expect nothing less from my friend and teammate for life: Mike Palma!"

Jeff Ruland Two-time NBA All-Star, Washington Bullets

"Mike Palma was a great player at St. Agnes. I attended rival Holy Trinity. The Agnes/Trinity rivalry was as intense as the Carolina/Duke rivalry I had the pleasure of being a part of as a player and coach. What I remember about Mike was he played so hard and was a geat shooter. He competed his tail off even when I saw him play in the playgrounds. I admired Mike a great deal—and I hated Mike—because he played for St. Agnes. When I was in seventh grade

I attended the Agnes/Trinity Long Island championship game. It was an intense battle. Agnes won and I remember walking out of the stands disappointed to see Mike cutting down the net. I took a Tootsie Roll out of my pocket and rifled it at him. Fortunately, I missed.

Fast forward forty-five years. Mike and I connected on a monthly business webinar I was conducting. Mike was a regular participant often offering valuable insight. Some of those insights are detailed in this book, *Walk with a Humble Swagger*. My respect for him soared as he demonstrated great wisdom and compassion. I am forever a Mike Palma fan. A man I hated, I now greatly admire."

Matt Doherty Former Head Coach University of Notre Dame and University of North Carolina

"As a young copywriter at a red-hot small agency, I got a call that changed my life. A guy named Michael Palma wanted to talk about an opportunity—selling me on an agency called Leonard/Monahan to replace this guy named David Lubars who recently left. In truth, I knew exactly who they were. I was just a copywriter, not a creative director; but this job was to be a partner and CD of the whole thing, skipping over five to 10 years of career.

Michael, with his eye for up-and-coming talent, somehow sold them on seeing me. Then he walked us all through the process of hiring a completely green, but enormously ambitious creative person, into a new level of career at one of the best small agencies in the country. I owe a lot to that first phone call and all his calls thereafter. I thank Michael every day for making it."

David Baldwin Founder, Baldwin&

"I arrived in Worcester, Massachusetts at Holy Cross in the early 1980s from rural Vermont, desperate to make a mark in Div. I hoops. Palms, an assistant coach who could still really play and regularly beat my ass in full court one-on-ones, would then spend hours with me, critically breaking down my game and detail what I had to do to actually be successful. These weren't 'rah rah try harder' BS speeches, they were intricate perspectives as to what I actually had to change, develop, and refine to be an impact player. We had teams that punched above our weight, and had a 'circle the wagons' mentality that reflected Palma's and our coaching staff's values.

Equally important, he instilled in me, a mentality of *Fuck it, you're as good or better as any of these guys you are playing against.* Yep, it's that humble swagger that I most appreciate. His success, while impressive, is a reflection of a work ethic and unique insight that make our hoops and business community a more vibrant cosmos!"

Jim McCaffrey Holy Cross player, New England Basketball Hall of Fame

"Mike is absolutely one of a kind. I worked with him on three reviews and no one knows people and agencies better. He is a super thoughtful and loving individual. He is someone you can bounce any challenge or idea off of, or simply talk life.

During my tenure as an adjunct professor at Boston University, Mike was my first call to guest speak. He led an insightful session on career paths with his 'arc of a great career' philosophy. It was the highlight of the course and an inspiration for us all to reach that 'vocation' status."

Linda SanGiacomo Chief Marketing Officer, Jordan's Furniture

"Recruiting requires as much poise and accuracy as an alley-oop pass with no time left on the clock. The lives that he has impacted both on and off the court are a testament to his character and unbridled passion to make great things happen. Our conversations throughout the years have always left me feeling inspired about our business and the untapped potential of it all. He always makes you feel like you are part of something so much bigger. That no challenge is too big or too audacious to overcome.

This book is a treasure trove of industry knowledge, truth, and empathy. Dive into that trove with a hunger and heart like no other. You'll find Michael at the center of it all. Ready to share his wisdom while helping you discover the greater swagger within."

David Angelo Founder and Creative Chairman, David&Goliath and Founder of Today, I'm Brave

"Mike's journey reminds me of the very significant role athletics can play in someone's life. His transition from a young Iona player when I first met him, to a successful executive, showcases the skills that can be linked between two different career paths. *Walk with a Humble Swagger* illustrates a great life lesson, told eloquently by Mike. I highly recommend it for anyone navigating through career choices."

Linda Bruno Bruno Sports Enterprises, Former Commissioner of the Atlantic 10 Conference and Former Associate Commissioner of the Big East

WALK WITH A HUMBLE SWAGGER

MICHAEL PALMA

Lessons From the Recruiting Trail
in Basketball and Advertising

Ripples Media

Published by Ripples Media
www.ripples.media

First printing 2024

Designed by Burtch Hunter

ISBN 979-8-9912870-1-2 Paperback
ISBN 979-8-9912870-2-9 Hardback
ISBN 979-8-9912870-0-5 E-book

WHY THIS IS THE MOST IMPORTANT BOOK YOU WILL EVER READ

Walk with a Humble Swagger might help you grow your business, accelerate your career, or even refocus your brand if you are in the advertising/marketing industry. It might also provide some inspiration to tackle the daily grind, a ray of hope and motivation. But, most importantly, simply by buying this book, you will help save children's lives.

Thirty percent of all proceeds from *Walk with a Humble Swagger* goes to the Dick Vitale Pediatric Cancer Research Fund at The V Foundation, whose founder Jim Valvano is a key figure in the pages that follow. As one of my mentors, a part of this book is tethered to his influence on my life.

Certainly, losing Coach V to cancer at the age of forty-six was a big blow. But it wasn't until 2018, when I lost my twin sister Michelle that cancer impacted my family. In 2019, The Palma Group made helping to cure cancer a key part of our mission.

Our 30th Anniversary Party in 2019 doubled as a fundraiser for the V Foundation. We subsequently did a lot of pro bono work for the Foundation with Connelly Partners, a great Boston-based agency.

Enjoy this book with the assurance that as you read each page, you are helping to fund research that will save lives.

Walk with a Humble Swagger is dedicated to the loving memory of my twin sister, Michelle Palma Furchak.

CONTENTS

Fifty years ago, I walked into the Palma living room as Coach Dick Vitale from the University of Detroit to recruit Mike Palma, a *Parade Magazine* All-American basketball player at St. Agnes High School in Rockville Centre, Long Island, to play for me. I recruited him with all of the passion I had because I knew he was one of legendary Coach Frank Morris's true superstars.

But I learned early on that talent alone is not enough to get the best recruit. You have to look beyond the players' stats to determine their work ethic, how they operate under pressure, and whether they have heart.

By sitting down with Mike's dad (Mike Sr.) in their living room, I knew I had to start there to find out what kind of person Mike was beyond the basketball court. Two Italian guys sharing our family heritage and the love of basketball, I knew I had won his dad over. I built what I thought was a great relationship and told them that I would see their son succeed on the court and in life.

Well, I lost this recruit to Wake Forest University and later to my dear friend, Coach Valvano, at Iona. You win some and you lose some. But now fifty years later, the one who got away is authoring a book about taking basketball recruiting lessons and converting them into executive recruiting skills.

Mike has a long history with basketball. He finished his playing career with Coach V and teammate Jeff Ruland at Iona, which went 29-5 and landed in the top 20. Although Mike did not play professional basketball, he always knew he wanted to coach. He coached a high school team for a few years and then moved on to recruit for Coach George Blaney at Holy Cross. Mike loved recruiting, loving all those hours in gymnasiums, diners, and motels on the road.

Like me, Mike had to finesse his recruiting skills traveling from home to home and from high school to high school. Those long road hours fine-tuned our approach to being better scouts, how to assess potential, establish trust, fit a player into a team, pivot when a player declines and be the best negotiator possible.

Mike took those basketball recruiting skills and made a change in 1989 and became one of the top executive recruiters in the country. He has placed over 1,500 ad agency executives. Mike learned early on that the competition in executive recruiting is just as intense as any rivalry on the court. Every coach is vying for the same talent. Heck, I was competing with Coach Boeheim, Cremins, Pitino and Tacy to get Mike. Every coach and every recruiter has to bring their A game every day to get the best of the best. But it is that trust, hard work, and passion that brings in those superstar players and turns them into a championship team.

Mike does that every day; building top ad agency teams that employ hundreds of thousands of employees across the country and around the globe.

This book, *Walk with a Humble Swagger,* is all about taking these recruiting skills and coupling the passion and the drive, and applying them to building a winning team in the business world.

In memory of his favorite Coach Valvano and his beloved twin sister, Michelle, who passed away from cancer twenty-five years apart, and in honor of the V Foundation for Cancer Research's work in pediatric cancer research Mike and Ripples Media are donating 30% of the proceeds of this book to the Dick Vitale Pediatric Cancer Research Fund at The V Foundation. I may not have won Mike Palma the recruit, but I sure won Mike Palma the man for the Vitale team to fight for the kids who have cancer!

Yes, Mike is a winner in the GAME OF LIFE and is AWESOME BABY with a Capital "A!"

DICK VITALE

ESPN BASKETBALL ANALYST AND MEMBER OF
THE COLLEGE BASKETBALL HALL OF FAME

INTRODUCTION

Why this book exists

In the winter of 2009, I wrote my first blog post for mikepalma.com. I was newly divorced with a lot of newfound time on my hands. In a rented three-story brownstone in Inman Park, I took to the keyboard armed with a desire to share lessons learned in big-time basketball and advertising, my two distinctly separate professional careers.

The "why" for the blog was the mikepalma.com tagline: "helping creative people, agencies, and brands grow." Its mission was and still is to provide valuable free content to this niche audience, which essentially consists of my clients and prospects. I made the conscious decision to write—to be a "blogger."

But, beneath the obvious business goal exposure, the real "why" of the blog that compelled and inspired my writing was something simpler—my ego.

A lot of writers say that writing is "cathartic." I'm not sure what catharsis is, but I know it was ego-boosting to create a post and instantly publish it online. It was a rush to see how, where, and by whom it was consumed and engaged with in real time, through the analytics of WordPress.

And then I wrote another blog post. And then another. Then another. And before long, I was overcome by dopamines feeding the addiction to having my "stuff" read and appreciated. The statistics were overwhelming and encouraging. I quickly created a community of advertising and marketing professionals hungry for the next post. One post alone, "How to Attract & Retain Top Talent," garnered over 10,000 subscribers to the blog.

Much of this book is a compilation of those posts, particularly the ones focusing on ad agency growth through business development and recruiting top talent. In fact this book's title, *Walk with a Humble Swagger,* was born in an early blog post "Evaluating Talent." And there are a number of posts dedicated to the advertising creative community at large.

"Writing a book" is not what I set out to do. I just wanted to write another blog post as soon as possible. And then have people tell me how clever and funny I was. Agency leaders emailed me to say the content really helped them rethink their agency and the ad business. They said it helped them make better choices, hire better people, and get better clients. Brand leaders reached out to thank me for insights in helping them hire an agency.

Other agency owners said they just read a post and didn't know what to make of it. I took both types of responses as a compliment.

This effort came off the heels of the 4A's (American Association of Advertising Agencies) rejecting my manuscript entitled *Best Practices for Ad Agency Recruiting: How to Attract & Retain Top Talent* in 2008. The gentleman, now retired, heading the 4A's Talent Committee said the content was "too irreverent." It was.

But I felt I'd rather be irreverent than irrelevant. And it was more authentic to the persona I created as an agency headhunter and rainmaker for twenty years up to that point. Irreverence is the Palma Persona (I don't usually refer to myself in the third person, I'll try not to do it again). It's one of the traits that gave me "phone cred" with creative directors, copywriters and art directors—the primary roles we recruit for. They're an irreverent lot.

So, I had some rejected content from the 4A's manuscript. And I had forty years of stories as a blue-chip basketball recruit, then a recruiter of blue-chip student-athletes, and then finally as a recruiter of top-tier creative and strategic people for the best ad agencies in America.

My best business case study in the 1990s was the Miami-based agency Crispin & Porter. I placed employee number eighteen. Then number twenty-one. Then a whole slew of creative and account service folks, most notably Bill Wright. I worked directly with Alex Bogusky and Chuck Porter. I was lucky to help them become The Agency of the Decade in the 1990s. Dumb luck. Right place, right time.

Our second significant business success story in the 1990s was GSD&M in Austin, Texas. I placed employee number forty, an art director named David Crawford from McKinney & Silver in Raleigh. He only lasted thirty years at the agency. I moved dozens of creative people to Austin—which was then a one-agency town—on GSD&M's journey from 40 to 400 employees. Guy Bommarito, like Bogusky, was a great client who had faith in my ability even before I did. I've been close friends with both Guy and Alex for years. My career became inextricably linked to their success.

In this century, Tombras Group, based in Knoxville, is our strongest case study. We helped Charlie and Dooley Tombras triple in size (from 150 employees to 450) and become *Ad Age*'s Independent Agency of the Year in 2024. Dumb luck. Right place, right time.

The blog really drove business to my company, The Palma Group, to the point where we now do a lot of things beyond recruiting. It attracted new agency clients literally from Portland, Maine, to Portland, Oregon. We were able to expand our business offerings into an ecosystem of services that drove our clients' growth. We established expertise in agency business development. Mikepalma.com organically created new revenue streams. We were already renowned as the premier ad agency headhunting firm. But the blog helped us be so much more. It diversified our company.

Maybe most importantly, the blog brought us our first Agency Reviews. Companies like Heineken, Coca-Cola, Fender, Yamaha, and Arby's asked me if I'd be interested in helping them identify creative partners. Could I help them manage their RFP process? I never woke up one day and made a conscious decision to do that. Those brands found me somehow through mikepalma.com. The first one told me, "you seem to know more about the agencies out there than our last search consultant did—can you help us?"

All this because one day I wrote a blog post and was overcome by ego and vanity to write more.

I could have just gone on headhunting forever and been perfectly happy. But the community we created through mikepalma.com drove the demand for us to do so much more for our agency clients. We were able to leverage what I learned from my time at BBDO as SVP and Director of Business Development (2003-2006). It made sharing new business lessons from Madison Avenue easy. As a result, we became our own supply chain; and to this day:

- We get brands the best agency partner
- We get agencies new business
- We get agencies top talent to service new business
- Rinse, wash, repeat

In hindsight, it's easy to see how I grew up to become a recruiter. I learned the art from some of the greatest recruiters of all time: John Thompson, Rick Pitino, Jim Boeheim, Dick Vitale, Lou Carnesecca, Dean Smith, Bobby Cremins, Frank McGuire, Bill Raftery, Jim Valvano. Those guys personally recruited me as a teenager. They all came to our house on Long Island and sat in our living room. I learned every pitch, every close, every persuasion, every trick and gimmick by the time I was eighteen years old. This book contains stories and anecdotes from those encounters.

Walk with a Humble Swagger morphs into a business book from the cocoon of a basketball book. It's a metamorphosis, a transformation—the book and my life. It's a coming-of-age story—a bildungsroman.

It was only natural to try and emulate these larger-than-life icons in my own career. Without even considering any other career, I became a basketball coach following my playing career. Coaching chose me, I was powerless.

At Holy Cross College I developed a knack and a reputation for signing student-athletes. It's easy to transfer these skills to headhunting for ad agencies. It's actually easier to recruit executives than teenagers. There are no NCAA rules. No limits to conversations, visits, lunches, or entertainment. If I want to pay a recruit a signing bonus from my fee to get a deal done, I do. There are no sanctions or death penalties.

This book is a collection of lessons I've learned as a recruiter, both in the basketball and the advertising worlds. While these are two areas that don't necessarily overlap conventionally, in both cases recruiting talent is the lifeblood of success.

These skills honed as a basketball coach helped prepare me to be Senior Vice President, Director of Business Development for one of the largest advertising agencies in the world, BBDO. Biz Dev *is* recruiting. You are recruiting clients in similar ways to recruiting employees.

As different as the two industries appear to be, I've always approached my advertising work with the mentality of a college basketball coach—incorporating the same principles of wooing talented student-athletes to recruiting extraordinarily talented ad agency people or prospective clients.

- Develop a meaningful relationship
- Understand the prospect's goals
- Don't sell them until you can fulfill a need
- Close on the true benefit

Hey, I had a pretty good nine-year run as a basketball coach. Consecutive state championships as a high school head coach. Then six years as a Division I assistant. Holy Cross was a special place for a young man to be. The alumni network was powerful: Bob Cousy, Tom Heinsohn, Justice Clarence Thomas, Edward Bennett Williams, Dr. Anthony Fauci, and Bill Simmons, to name a few. It was hallowed ground.

And I've been lucky to have an amazing run as *kind of* an ad guy: working closely with legends like David Lubars, Lee Clow, Hal Riney, Tom Monahan, David Baldwin, Paul Cappelli, Alex Bogusky, Andrew Robertson, Chuck Porter, David Angelo and Charlie Tombras.

You'd think I'd be tired of advertising—but I love the business now more than ever. And that's because today I'm fortunate to work with the next generation of legends: Eric Kallman, Dooley Tombras, Steve Erich, Paul Venables, Duff Stewart, John Vitro, David Oakley and Chris Jacobs.

Maybe what I'm most grateful for, are our agency-owner clients who have become dear, lifelong friends—Curtis

Zimmerman, Steve Connelly, Tommy Luckie, Kurt Tausche, Patrick Scullin, Tinsley Van Durand, Rob Farinella, Michael Pavone, Dave Fitzgerald, Ed Klein, Dan Dodson, Michael Brunner, Jeff Maggs, Alex Van Winkle and Joe Johnson.

I thought about publishing this book about ten years ago. But it felt premature and undercooked. I felt like I was too young to release a collection of essays like this. It's like wearing a bow tie. You have to be old to wear a bow tie, or you'll look like a dork. Business books are that way for me.

Walk with a Humble Swagger is allegorical. The journey itself is both literal and a metaphor.

This is a different kind of book. There are lots of basketball books written by and about coaches and players much better than I ever was. Of all those, I was most influenced by *Life On the Run* by Bill Bradley.

And there are a lot of advertising books about the industry and New Business. I was greatly influenced by Cleve Langton's *New Business Lessons from Madison Avenue*.

Safe to say, neither of those books is a bildungsroman.

But there are no hybrid basketball/advertising books. Until now. Thanks for suffering through the intro. It can only get better from here...

With that in mind, who is this book specifically for?

AD AGENCY OWNERS

Particularly owners of mid-sized, independent regional creative agencies. That's the audience that may most benefit from reading this book. My stuff is better suited to the mavericks. The irreverent persona plays better to the underdogs. Not that the global, monolithic holding company executive commuting from the Connecticut suburbs won't snicker at some of this content. These lessons apply most directly to the challenges of the mid-major owners and, often, founders. This book serves as a field guide for the startup business neophytes as well as a survival guide for seasoned mavericks fighting the good fight.

THE AD AGENCY CREATIVE COMMUNITY

Creative directors, Associate Creative Directors, Chief Creative Officers, Executive Creative Directors, Copywriters, and Art Directors. These posts are chock-full of leadership and career tips. These folks represent at least one-third of The Palma Group's 1,500 agency placements. Those are the roles we built our company and brand on. That's the core of our business. Creative leadership is kind of an oxymoron. It requires both an acute sensitivity to the human condition as well as an emotional fascist temperament. That's the voice of this book. The Palma Group does a lot of things, but everything we do hinges upon the sole ability to sell creative solutions. Creative people (and leaders) will learn how to do that better after reading this book.

NEW BUSINESS/BUSINESS DEVELOPMENT AGENCY PEOPLE

It takes a sick mind to choose ad agency new business as a career path. Shoot, it takes a sick mind to be in the ad agency business, period.

New business folks have the hardest job in advertising. The rejection rate is staggering. The sales cycle is glacial. They get no credit for the wins and all the blame for the losses. This book requires a bit of a peculiar mindset from the reader.

Sometimes the reader will feel as if they are rubbernecking an accident on the interstate. But there are so many winning lessons contained within these pages that I learned from thousands of pitches while sitting on both sides of the table: agency-side and consultant-for-client-side.

HR PROFESSIONALS, RECRUITERS AND TALENT ACQUISITION PEOPLE

The recruiting content in this book has great benefits for Talent Acquisition folks, particularly those in service industries. There are tips and tactics that are sure to help recruiters improve their skills and performance.

CURIOUS OUTSIDERS

My guess is about 15% of our readers have nothing to do with advertising. They love basketball history or sports in general. There's a lot of content in this book to keep those folks entertained as well. Many stories contained herein glorify the golden age of college basketball. The two sections following this Introduction should satisfy that reader. However, this audience should be forewarned that the vernacular beyond the prologue is heavy-duty advertising-speak.

THE ELEMENTS OF STYLE GUIDE

In the blog posts, as the narrator of this chronicle of the past thirty-five years of advertising agency life, I try to assume the character and voice of Nick Carraway, the humble but omniscient center of *The Great Gatsby*.

I also borrow and steal greatly from the journalistic style of legendary New York tabloid columnist Jimmy Cannon.

The tone is often mock-heroic, emulating Geoffrey Chaucer's *Nun's Priest Tale*. I'm Chauntecleer, parodying the subjects and then exaggerating the trivialities.

There are a few times when the posts transform into actual heroism. We battle cancer much like Beowulf confronted Grendel. Posts such as "The Arc of Great Career" and "Advertising in the Garden of Good and Evil" are hero's tales. After I finished writing them, I had the rare and unfamiliar feeling that, deep down, I was a good guy. That feeling never lasted very long.

The Prologue (basketball section) borrows somewhat from the Amory Blaine character in Fitzgerald's *This Side of Paradise*. And probably a little bit of Ted Williams' *My Turn at Bat*.

That's not to say it's all smooth sailing and easy reading. If this book was a music genre, it wouldn't be "Easy Listening." It would sound a little bit like a Tom Waits outtake—experimental and at times unnerving.

Really smart people in the publishing business have read the blog and had no idea what to make of it. I took that as a compliment. It moves fast. It's not for the faint of heart. If it were a movie, it would be in black and white, not technicolor—and the film would be a little grainy.

As you will see, many posts deploy the popular blogging technique of "Listicles." They are structured in the inverted pyramid format: a few intro paragraphs, the bullets (lists) and one or two brief closing paragraphs. I wanted the posts to be scanable and feel unthreatening in their consumption time—"two-minute read" kind of stuff. Quick pops. The most exciting two minutes in advertising, like the Kentucky Derby of advertising commentary.

I'd love to someday read the posts aloud with violin accompaniment.

Mostly, I strove to "make language new," as this is what W.H. Auden claimed to be the writer's duty. I often referred to Strunk & White just to remind myself of the importance of the elements of style. The posts themselves aspire to be properly written. I try not to take poetic license, which I consider cheating. There's a Salinger parody and a Jay McInerny parody, but everything else is pretty much me, stylistically.

While I was influenced by Jimmy Cannon, Chaucer, Fitzgerald and Tom Waits, I knew I still had to speak in my own voice and it had to be colorful and different. The best mikepalma.com posts reflect that concerted effort. I hope.

Prologue

HOW BASKETBALL PREPARED ME
FOR A LIFE IN ADVERTISING

In January 1968, I remember staying up late to watch the UCLA vs. Houston game, billed the "Game of the Century." It was the first college basketball game I ever saw, televised by the TVS Television Network, a broadcast network that has been defunct for thirty years but was an early syndicate of American sports programming. It was also the first nationally televised college basketball game in prime time, and there were doubts back then that America would tune in for an amateur product. These days, television rights fees for the major conferences in football and basketball go for a couple of billion dollars. TVS paid $27,000 for broadcast rights for the 1968 Game of the Century in the Astrodome.

Although UCLA lost (they wouldn't lose again until 90 games later), my life changed that evening. When broadcaster Dick Enberg said that all these players on television received full college scholarships to *play basketball*—well, that provided me with my first true goal. I was going to be one of those guys someday on TV playing basketball and getting a full college scholarship. It was a few days before my eleventh birthday and I just knew deep inside that it would happen.

I loved Lew Alcindor (now known as Kareem Abdul-Jabbar). He hailed from my native New York City-area Catholic school league and he was inordinately tall (I was a 6-foot-3 sixth grader at the time). I even copied his hook shot. Alcindor was my first basketball idol. He was eloquent and opinionated, but respectful of the game and his coaches. His 1969 autobiographical *Sports Illustrated* article, "My Story" provided me with my first glimpse into Coach John Wooden, the greatest coach of all time. From that moment on, I read and watched everything I could about the man who first inspired me to choose coaching as my first career out of college.

SACRED HEART SCHOOL

I was born in Coney Island, Brooklyn, home of Nathan's Famous. That might explain why I was such a hot dog. It was the year the Dodgers left Brooklyn. My family lived in a basement apartment in Sheepshead Bay, an enterprise fishing enclave across from Coney Island. The town obviously had a fishy smell. Vince Lombardi was from Sheepshead Bay. So is Larry David, by the way (which explains a lot about my personality and the fishy smell says a lot about his facial expression).

When I was four years old, thanks to the New York State Highway Planning Commission led by Robert Moses, we moved out to the suburbs on Long Island along with millions of other Brooklyn families. We lived a few miles from Jones Beach. Our social, spiritual and academic lives were tethered to the Catholic Church in our town—Sacred Heart Church.

My first basketball team was at Sacred Heart Elementary School in Merrick, NY; Nassau County on Long Island. My first coaches were two really tough but wonderful men, and my teammates' fathers: Jack Johnston and Denny McCann. Good cop and bad cop.

My father saved Mr. McCann's life when Denny had a heart attack at practice. My dad was the only parent there in the park and he rushed him to the hospital. Mr. McCann took time off from the NYPD and in his recovery, he completely devoted his life to our basketball team.

I had a gift as an extremely tall manchild with a pro-clivity of putting a basketball through a hoop. My dad was a great athlete—he won a full baseball scholarship to Long Island University where he played for the legendary coach Clair Bee (Bee was also a prolific author of wonderful sports books). My dad was a tall, wiry lefty with a sweet swing like Ted Williams. I inherited his athletic genes and hand-eye coordination. Great shooters must have great hands. Born lucky, I had them.

I was an excitable boy as a youngster—incredibly high-strung and driven. I put a lot of pressure on myself. My dad would drive me to practices and see me nervously fidgeting in the car, unable to sit still. Every practice seemed to be a quest for perfection. I had difficulty accepting less. I remember my dad dropping me off at the gym for practice and simply say-ing, "just do your best." He was always so calm and rational. Those are words I live by to this day and the core of my paren-tal guidance with my own children. Do your best. I'm lucky to have such a great father.

By the time I was twelve years old, as somewhat of a grammar school basketball phenom on Long Island, it felt like all eyes in my community were upon me. A 6-foot-3 adolescent freak, I literally stood head and shoulders above any crowd of my peers. There was no hiding for me.

Most kids get to grow up in relative anonymity. Every Parish in Nassau County seemed to know who I was. Bernie Beglane, a sportswriter for the *Long Island Catholic*, a weekly newspaper with a large circulation, wrote a full column about me. Among the platitudes and achievements, he speculated where I might attend high school. I was twelve years old and already facing external pressure within our community to attend a half-dozen or so high schools.

Looking back, I may have peaked at twelve years old.

A few high school coaches were already recruiting me in seventh grade. I felt like I was growing up in public; with little margin for social error.

I was lucky to play at Sacred Heart for Mr. Johnston and Mr. McCann. We had a great tradition. We hardly ever lost. I can only recall losing four games in three years. Two notable Sacred Heart Hoops Alums are Bob McKillop, who coached Steph Curry at Davidson and Kevin Joyce. Kevin played on the 1972 USA Olympic team that got screwed by the refs in Munich in the famous game against Russia (then known as USSR). McKillop and Joyce paved the way for me as a fledgling hoopster.

A fourteen-year-old Palma posts up New York hoops legend
Beaver Smith in a Summer League game prior to his
freshman year at St. Agnes.

ST. AGNES HIGH SCHOOL

I decided to attend the fabled St. Agnes Cathedral High School in Rockville Centre, N.Y. It was the best high school basketball program on Long Island. The most renowned St. Agnes players are Frankie Alagia and a kid named Billy Donovan, who went on to coach the University of Florida to back-to-back national titles and currently coaches the NBA's Chicago Bulls. But there were dozens of great Stags who played college basketball. Jimmy Hayes is still the all-time leading scorer at Boston University. Same with John Batule at Biscayne. Peter Crotty played for Digger Phelps at Notre Dame. Eddie Molloy was 5'5" tall and started at the University of Rhode Island. The Mahoney Brothers, Brian and Charlie, both starred at Manhattan College. Brian succeeded Lou Carnessecca as head coach at St. John's. I was lucky to be part of that tradition too. So many great players and winners.

On Winter Friday evenings, St. Agnes Basketball filled whatever gymnasium we played in. We were more than a basketball team; we were an attraction. We were also polarizing, kind of like the Yankees. People either loved us or hated us. We outdrew Hofstra in their own arena. When we played before a college basketball game in Nassau Coliseum as part of a doubleheader, half the crowd would leave after our game. We'd do shooting exhibitions at halftime of Dr. J's Nets games at Nassau Coliseum.

I played on the varsity team all four years, the first player to do that in school history. We never lost a home game. Never. We hardly ever lost at all. We were 74-18 in my four seasons.

The St. Agnes Stags scheduled prestigious programs like DeMatha, Archbishop Molloy and Long Island Lutheran regularly. We played against John Thompson's St. Anthony's team in Washington, DC. We played and beat the best.

In my first high school game in a St. Agnes uniform in December 1971, we played one of the greatest high school teams of all time, Mount Vernon, at Hofstra University. They had four future NBA players in Gus and Ray Williams, Earl Tatum, and Rudy Hackett. We won 71-69. I think it was the greatest win in the history of Long Island high school basketball.

A few weeks later, we played DeMatha in the Long Island Holiday Festival. In the first quarter, I took Adrian Dantley out to the corner and drilled a jumper. Then next time down the court Frankie Alagia got me the ball in the same spot and

I drilled another. Morgan Wooten, the legendary DeMatha coach called a timeout and I could hear him yelling at Dantley that I was "only a freshman." In the huddle, I told Frankie "next time down I'm going back door." And I did. Frankie hit me with a perfect bounce pass. Six points in one minute against the best high school player in America. I was thirteen years old.

Later that week, I received my first recruiting letter. It was written on bright orange stationary from the University of Tennessee and signed by a guy named Stu Aberdeen, an amazing recruiter. He recruited me steadily over the next four years, as did dozens of other great coaches. It started right after that DeMatha game in 1971 and never let up until the spring of 1975.

On most days, I played basketball for four hours. But on others, I played for seven or eight hours. I shot five hundred shots every day; an arsenal of different shots. I'd practice them in imaginary game situations every day. Basketball players and creative advertising people are similar in that they both need grandiose imaginations to be good. They both need to "visualize" success.

I got such a rush becoming a great shooter. Those dopamines drove me. I wanted to someday walk down the street and have people say, "there goes the greatest shooter I ever saw." I was fourteen years old. I was a little punchy and with a bunch of swagger, but not much humble. It takes a certain foolish naïveté to be exceptional. I was a lucky fool.

My coach, Frank Morris, was a real character—a legend. He was Mr. Morris, we never called him "Coach." In my four years I don't recall him ever calling a timeout. His St. Agnes system ran on the "four-second offense." We played basketball at a breakneck pace, routinely breaking the 100-point mark in our 32-minute games without the three-point line. Think about that. That's why we were an attraction, like the Harlem Globetrotters.

Morris' style of play somewhat artificially inflated my stats. Thirty-to-40-point games were common for me. I even went for 51 points one night in my junior year—the school record. Frankie Alagia said if there were a 3-point line, I would have had 70. Our gym was a bandbox and I got up 20 to 30 shots per game. Three steps over halfcourt and it went up. And they usually went in.

It was a perfect storm—the St. Agnes system, my compulsive egomaniacism and the luck to play with four incredibly savvy point guards.

FRANK ALAGIA Frankie subsequently had four great years at St. John's. At 5'9" he won the Francis Pomeroy Naismith Award as America's best player under 6 feet. He took me under his wing when I was a freshman. I was lucky to break into big-time high school basketball and get to play with maybe the best point guard in the history of Long Island.

KEVIN CROUTIER Kevin is a SUNY-Oneonta Hall of Famer. He still holds the all-time assists record there. He drove me , like a jockey riding a racehorse.

MIKE MILLER I've said, "Mike Miller made me an All-American," because the Junior year is what the scouts base their rankings upon. He got me at least 20 shots every game as a Junior. He made me quicker and tougher. He was so tough he took a basketball scholarship to Kent State in the Four-Dead-in-Ohio mid-1970's.

ROB CONROY Rob got me the ball on every possession. That's all. But, more than basketball, Rob was the first literary influence on my life. We were both voracious readers and fledgling writers. Maybe the most important thing Rob did for me was expose me to Bob Dylan. On my 18th birthday, after a Friday night game, we sat speechless in his room and listened to WNEW-FM preview "Blood on the Tracks" in its entirety. I was never really the same person again.

Mr. Morris' practices often ran for three to four hours. We were the best-conditioned team on the East Coast. He ran us ragged with full-court drills. We'd shoot jump shots for about an hour every practice. He'd absolutely berate and humiliate us for hours in the privacy of the practice gym. But, he had the discipline to calmly sit through our games, never getting up from the bench—never embarrassing us in front of our friends and family. That's what I admired about him most. He maintained his grace and dignity in public. In private, Mr. Morris was a raging lunatic. But he was able to harness that energy and sit sphinx-like in the heat of battle.

He was the most competitive person I've ever been around—and I've been around thousands of high-achieving competitors in both basketball and advertising. You'll read about a lot of competitive people in this book, but none were more so than Frank Morris.

My favorite story illustrating his competitiveness took place at Rockville Links Club in Rockville Centre in the late 1990s, almost forty years after I first played basketball for him. I walked into the men's grill after playing 18 holes with my dad. Mr. Morris was walking out. We hadn't seen each other for at least fifteen years. We shook hands and said hello. He immediately asked me what score I shot on the course. I told him I carded an 80 with three birdies. Without my asking, he said, "I shot 79 with four birdies." He said he had to head out and it was great to see me again. It was the last time I saw him before he died in 2004.

I then walked into the men's grill and saw a bunch of my old high school buddies hanging out. I said, "Hey it was great to see Mr. Morris—he must have played pretty well." One of my St. Agnes buddies said, "What? He shot like a 120. He's terrible. And he never stops talking—even during your backswing and while you're putting."

Largely because of Frank Morris' system, one of the greatest coaches in high school basketball history, I was fortunate to be named to the *Parade Magazine* All-American Team in 1975.

Street & Smith's Basketball Annual (the leading publication of the time) put me in their top 10 of high school All-Americans alongside Daryl Dawkins and Bill Cartwright.

How lucky could a kid get? From a basement apartment in Brooklyn to one of the top 10 high school basketball players in the country.

The ridiculous numbers I put up in Frank Morris' system at St. Agnes led to the publicity which led to being really heavily recruited by dozens of big-time college programs. Syracuse, Georgetown, Tennessee, Florida, Holy Cross, UNC, Duke, Wake Forest in 1975.

These are some of the coaches who sat in our living room for visits and made their pitch for my basketball services:

Jim Boeheim—Syracuse
Rick Pitino—Hawaii
Dick Vitale—Detroit
Lou Carnesecca –St. John's
John Thompson—Georgetown
George Blaney—Holy Cross
John Bach—Penn State
Bill Foster—Duke
Carl Tacy—Wake Forest
Chuck Daly—Penn
Brendan Malone—Power Memorial HS
Bobby Cremins—South Carolina
Frank McGuire—South Carolina

Fred Schaus—Purdue

Eddie Fogler—North Carolina

Bill Raftery—Seton Hall

John Lotz—Florida

As the 1975 Long Island championship game MVP,
Palma had 22 points and 18 rebounds for St. Agnes.

WAKE FOREST UNIVERSITY

My final two choices came down to Duke and Wake Forest. Duke was really bad at the time, like 8-20 bad. I wanted to go to Duke and average 28 per game as a freshman. Blue Devils coach Bill Foster was a fast-break guy. But, I had a better campus visit at Wake and they recruited really well. And, most importantly, they had better players than Duke.

The main reason I signed with Wake was an amazing guy named Neill McGeachy. He had a brief stint as interim head coach at Duke prior to joining Wake Forest. He was an incredible recruiter. As a result of his masterful job. I chose Wake. He was gone after my freshman year. The thing about luck is it comes in both good and bad. Coach McGeachy leaving the program was bad luck for me.

When I sat in the coaches offices during my campus visit at Duke, Bill Foster was talking on the phone and said, "Hang on Mike, someone wants to say hi to you." I took the phone and it was Jimmy Valvano who played for Foster at Rutgers. He cracked a few jokes and told me to sign with Duke.

If I had, I probably would not have wound up playing for him (we'll get to that in a minute).

My Wake Forest Demon Deacons beat Duke in Cameron Indoor Stadium by 39 points. If I had to endure many losses like that at Duke, I would have hung myself.

The following season, Gene Banks, as a freshman single-handedly turned the program around as Duke eventually played Kentucky in the 1978 national championship game. I would have played in that championship game.

Many years later, I ran into Bill Foster in an airport. He told me that if I went to Duke, they would have beaten Kentucky in that game and won the national championship. He said, "Kentucky packed in a zone around Gminski and Banks with their two 7-footers. We needed a shooter on the perimeter to loosen up their zone so we could get the ball inside."

It's easy to say now that I should have gone to Duke. But hindsight is 20/20. Overall, I had a good experience at Wake Forest. Who really knows what would have happened at Duke? But Foster's remark in the airport made me think.

In my first game in a Wake Forest uniform, I scored 37 points at Memorial Coliseum in Winston-Salem. No three-point line. A few weeks later, I was named ACC Rookie of the Week for my performance in the old Big Four Tournament (Duke, Wake, UNC, NC State, the ACC's four North Carolina schools). In January I went for 19 points in 22 minutes in Cole

Field House against Lefty Driesell's Maryland Terrapins. Even John Lucas couldn't stop me. I was on my way.

That summer, Wake recruited two guys, Frank Johnson and Leroy McDonald, who severely impacted my playing time. They were both great athletes who were very different players than me. Leroy could jump over the moon and Frank was already an NBA-level player as a freshman. He wound up playing in the NBA for some great Phoenix Suns teams and he eventually became the head coach of the franchise.

This was the first time in my basketball career in which someone was better and had more talent than I did. I learned a great lesson at Wake Forest that was applicable to my career in executive recruiting—everyone is replaceable with someone better. There's always someone better. When you're not practicing, they are.

I did get to an Elite Eight game the next season at Wake, the Midwest regional final in Oklahoma City in 1977. We were up at the half against eventual champion Marquette. But Al McGuire got to the refs at halftime and they blew us out in the second half. I was that close to a Final Four. The NCAA tournament in those days was a field of 32—half its current size. That team was really good and Rod Griffin and Skip Brown led us to a No. 9 ranking in the final AP poll.

Receiving considerably less playing time in 1977 compared to my freshman year. I decided to transfer back home. My over-inflated ego burst. If anything will put humble in your swagger, it's the sound of your ego popping like champagne bottles at midnight on New Year's Eve. The dopamine supply was depleted.

I went from making the ACC All-Rookie team as a freshman to being an also-ran on perhaps the best team in Wake Forest history, but an also-ran nevertheless. I had two years of eligibility left and I wanted to play.

I was changing jobs. The utter decisiveness of that action really informed my career as a headhunter. Living through that experience helped me advise thousands of advertising professionals faced with the reality of changing jobs. Little did I know it at the time, but transferring "jobs" would play a central role in my career in the advertising industry. Helping talented people through that process is a big part of what I do.

Duke was out as an option because the ACC had a rule against transferring in-conference (needless to say, the times have changed with player movement in the college transfer portal today). Almost certainly, I was going to transfer back home to New York and play for Lou Carnesecca at St. John's.

That is until my dad ran into Rocco Valvano, the athletic director at Seaford High School on Long Island. My dad sold sporting goods and team uniforms to the school districts. Rocco bought equipment for the Seaford teams from my Pop. He asked my dad, "How's the kid?"

My dad told him I was coming home and ready to enroll at St. John's. The elder Valvano told him his son Jimmy had recently taken the Iona job and just signed Jeff Ruland, who may be the best big man in Long Island history. Rocco called his son right then and there and told him he had Mike Palma's dad in his office and that I was planning to transfer from Wake Forest to St. John's. Of course, Jimmy V said, "He should have gone to Duke like I told him to." And then he asked my dad if he'd take me up to New Rochelle and visit Iona before signing with St. John's.

The author in his sophomore year at Wake Forest.

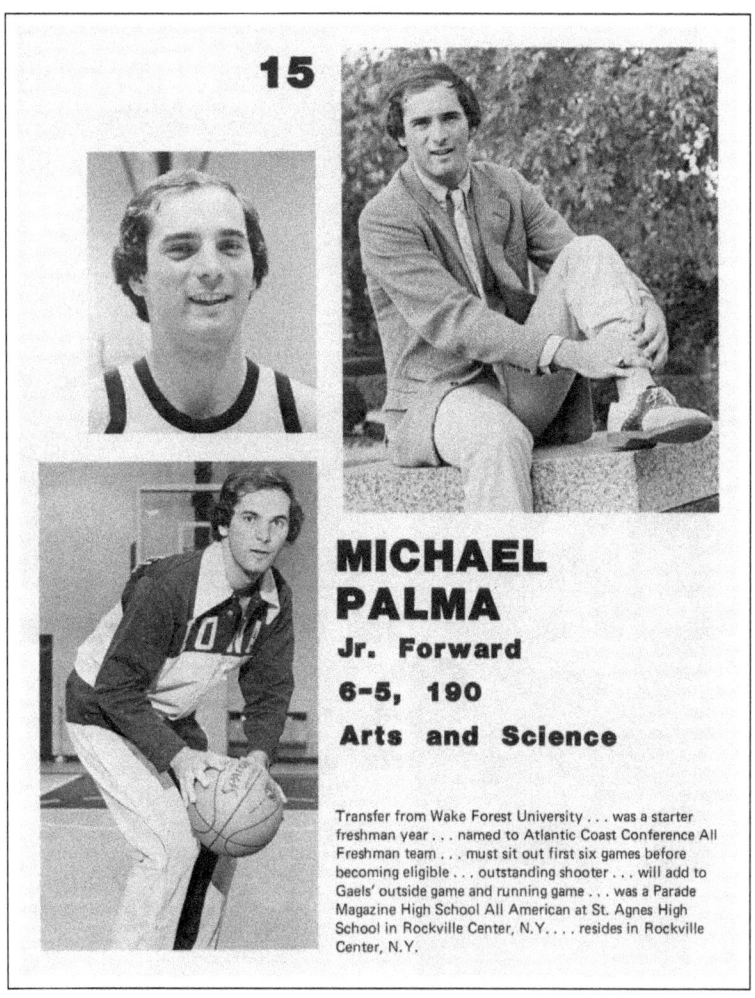

15

MICHAEL PALMA

Jr. Forward

6-5, 190

Arts and Science

Transfer from Wake Forest University . . . was a starter freshman year . . . named to Atlantic Coast Conference All Freshman team . . . must sit out first six games before becoming eligible . . . outstanding shooter . . . will add to Gaels' outside game and running game . . . was a Parade Magazine High School All American at St. Agnes High School in Rockville Center, N.Y. . . . resides in Rockville Center, N.Y.

The 1978-79 junior year at Iona College.

IONA COLLEGE

So a few days later, my dad and I drove up to Westchester County for the Iona-Detroit game. Detroit was coached by Dick Vitale. While Iona lost by one point, it was clear that all the Gaels needed was a zone-busting frontcourt shooter. Detroit had utilized a zone that sagged off to suffocate Jeff Ruland. However, with a corner shooter that could neutralize this defensive scheme, Iona could be really good, maybe even great. Ruland could be an All-American.

Valvano, or "Coach V," told me I was the missing piece to a top-20 team. He sold me on beating a national power in the 9 o'clock game in The Garden. Most of all, he sold me on daring to dream along with him, and doing it at a place it had never been done before. He sold me on how little Iona could be the king of New York City basketball. Even Ruland, who didn't like anybody, seemed to like me. I bought in and it was a life-changing decision.

Maybe the best thing that happened to me at Iona was I learned to become a team player. I wasn't a high scorer but instead, a key linchpin on two great championship teams. There are a lot of stars in New York, but there are few champions. If you look at the stats, mine are very ordinary at Iona. But, I played a key role, doing the little things, bringing mental toughness and a winning attitude. And in the big games down the stretch, when the team needed me to score, I did. Most importantly, I made my teammates better.

That's what great advertising people do—they win by making everyone around them better. Those are the kinds of people The Palma Group recruits today. Winners.

While that 1977 Elite 8 Wake Forest team was really good, our Iona 1980 team was perhaps even better. Even though we finished No. 19 in the final AP poll, we thought we were better than that. We beat Louisville, the eventual national champions, in Madison Square Garden 77-60 in one of the most memorable college games in New York City history. The contest snapped the Cardinals' 18-game winning streak. That game, in its entirety, can be found on YouTube under "Iona vs. Louisville 1980."

At Wake Forest and Iona, my college teams had a record of 91-29. Any time my team lost in either high school or college, I was absolutely shocked. I didn't know how to lose. If we did, it felt like a fluke. I got high on winning. Those dopamines drove me.

When I ask ad agency leaders what part of the business drives them the most, they almost always say "winning a pitch." The thrill of pitching and winning new business is the most direct correlation between agencies and basketball teams—a tangible win. In that way, coaching really helped set the stage for my career in agency new business. A pitch is a championship game.

Iona is a twenty-minute train ride to Midtown Manhattan. Being in New York in the late 1970s was such a glorious time. The city adopted our underdog team. And the city back in those days was crazy: Studio 54, Elaine's, Ryan McFadden's, Runyon's. We'd walk into a bar after a big game in the Garden, and we were like the Junior Knicks. I was lucky to be part of that. We were all lucky the legal age for drinking at the time was eighteen years old.

What a time we had, heading down to Chinatown after beating Kansas in the Garden with Coach V and the gang. Or going to Junior's in Brooklyn for cheesecake after a win against LIU in the old Paramount Theatre, recently converted into a basketball arena. Or having press conferences at Mama Leone's restaurant in Midtown on W. 48th Street. Or lunches at 21 Club with Iona alums. Everyone wanted us to attend their party.

It was all so simultaneously vivid and blurry, like a Ted Croner black-and-white photo from the 1940s. New York City was a grimy but glorious place in the '70s. We had Son of Sam in the headlines, making the entire city feel like a crime film noir. *Mean Streets* was more than a movie, it was the setting we lived in. We had the great Blackout in 1977, which was kind of a metaphor for the period.

We had emerging punk rock and new wave music as an outcry against disco. I would walk down the street in Manhattan and hear The Bee Gees' "Saturday Night Fever" on a boombox and on the next corner hear The Ramones' "End of the Century." We had Springsteen, Patti Smith and Lou Reed live at The Bottom Line for $5. We had Talking Heads and Blondie at CBGB's for a $2 cover charge. Ed Koch was Hizzoner. If we only had iPhones back then to capture it all. New York City was at the cutting edge of an international creative and cultural renaissance. And I was lucky to be smack dab in the middle of it.

It was a great two-year run. Iona Basketball caught lightning in a bottle from out of nowhere. Something like that could only happen in New York. It was the culmination of my playing career and everything I worked for. Five hundred jump shots a day. It took me ten years to become part of an overnight sensation.

We were New York City media darlings for a couple months in early 1980. The best team in the city on the back page of the New York tabloids every week—the *New York Post*, the *Daily News*. On the nightly sports news segments with Warner Wolf, Len Berman, Dick Schaap and Marv Albert.

I was interviewed and quoted in print by the greatest sportswriters of our generation: Mike Lupica, Tony Kornheiser, Leigh Montville, and Malcolm Moran.

The Iona Gaels were the kings of New York City college basketball. In a two-week span we beat both Kansas and Louisville in The Mecca of Basketball, Madison Square Garden.

This was New York City, not Winston-Salem, North Carolina. It was all so ephemeral and ethereal at the same time. It was like being a kid at Coney Island riding the Cyclone.

But, the ride always ends.

When my playing career ended in the Providence Civic Center against Sleepy Floyd's Georgetown team in March 1980, I knew I was going to pursue coaching as my next logical step. I felt like I was a natural-born leader—born and raised to coach.

At twenty-three years old, my body was worn down. I was like a car that only drove at 80 mph for eleven years. The engine was ground down. The treads on tires were worn. There was excess mileage on the odometer. Frank Morris's grueling system for four (formative) years, thousands of practices, dozens of sprained ankles, millions of jump shots, so much torque on such a young, wiry body. I never pursued professional basketball overseas. It was physically over. I wanted to be a coach. I was the oldest young man in America.

Palma during the 1979-80 year at Iona.

BISHOP McGUINNESS HIGH SCHOOL

After graduating from Iona, I got a call from a Wake Forest buddy about a head coach opening at a Catholic school back in Winston-Salem. It was Bishop McGuinness High School and they had a pretty strong basketball tradition. I got the job, and my coaching career got off to a flying start.

I put in Frank Morris' St. Agnes system at Bishop McGuinness and we won back-to-back state championships. We ran our opponents into the ground. I was the youngest coach in North Carolina high school basketball history to win consecutive state crowns. I had great kids from great families. They were so coachable and impressionable. And they worked as hard as I did a few years earlier at St. Agnes. I was so lucky to start my coaching career at Bishop McGuinness.

I also coached the varsity baseball team and taught six

tenth-grade English classes per day. My salary was $9,600 per year. In a lot of ways, those were the most rewarding three years of my life. I've somehow made a lot of money in my advertising career, but no amount of money can buy the memories I have as a high school basketball coach. It was a vocation. When I started treating my advertising career as a vocation, I once again felt similar gratification. But, that took many years of headhunting and new business.

All too often, we overly emphasize money and compensation as our end goal. We lose sight of why we chose our career path in the first place. When the only goal is chasing money, you will inevitably end up unfulfilled. As I look back, those early days of coaching Bishop McGuinness gave me a feeling of joy that still sticks with me forty years later. Let's remember why we first got into the business and seek opportunities that bring satisfaction and have nothing to do with a salary.

In 1981, I brought the Bishop McGuinness kids up to Long Island over Christmas break to play St. Agnes and Lutheran HS. Billy Donovan was Frank Morris' point guard. We lost 106-101. Thirty-two-minute game, no three-pointers. Lutheran's head coach was Bob McKillop. McKillop also played for Jack Johnston at Sacred Heart Elementary School. This basketball world is very small. Lutheran beat us too. However, we learned more from those two losses in New York than any games we could have won in North Carolina. We ran the table to the state championship the rest of the way once we returned to Winston-Salem.

The Bishop McGuinness Villains were invited to play in the Alhambra Catholic Invitational Tournament in Cumberland, Maryland. That tournament brought together the best Catholic high school teams on the East Coast. I drove the team up to Maryland in the school van.

As I pulled into the hotel parking lot, Morgan Wooten of DeMatha was parking his school's van next to ours. He walked over to me and said, "Coach Palma, congratulations on your team's success this season. Welcome to the Alhambra. I remember when you were a freshman at St. Agnes. You were one of the best young shooters I ever saw. Good luck in the tournament." That was one of the greatest things anyone ever said to me.

We won two games in the Alhambra. One of the many college coaches attending the tournament to evaluate recruits was George Blaney of Holy Cross. I visited Holy Cross while being recruited in high school and I really liked Coach Blaney, as you will learn in the upcoming chapter. At Iona, we played against Holy Cross in Madison Square Garden during my junior season, and then again in the NCAA tournament in 1980, where we played them in the game before we lost to Georgetown in Providence.

After spending some time with Coach Blaney in Maryland after a game, he asked me if I'd be interested in joining his Holy Cross coaching staff in Worcester, Massachusetts. I told him it would be a dream come true to be able to recruit great student-athletes for a school like The Cross. George hired me as full-time assistant basketball coach. My salary was $21,000 and all the Nike sneakers and apparel I could wear. In 1983, that was pretty cool. How lucky was I?

Jim Valvano's 1979-80 Iona Gaels team with #15 Mike Palma.

HOLY CROSS COLLEGE

We were an inaugural member of the Metro Atlantic Athletic Conference. The league was based in New York and most of the member institutions were in the New York metropolitan area—Fordham, Manhattan, Fairfield, St. Peter's, and Iona. It was fun to go back to Iona as a coach. As lead recruiter, I had my best success signing players from the Baltimore and D.C. area as well as metro New York. So I drove up and down the East Coast from Massachusetts to Northern Virginia like it was the Upper East Side of Manhattan.

Between going to our recruits' high school games, working premium summer camps like Five-Star, scouting our opponents, and the actual games themselves, I was on the road ten months per year. I was hardly ever home. In fact, I was in New York more than I was in Worcester. It was a whirlwind life. But I loved being on the road, Coach Mike Kerouac.

Recruiting, by far, is the single most important aspect of a college coach's job. Without good players, it's impossible to compete on the Division I level. The biggest key was recruiting the right players that fit into the system and the culture. This is the second-most correlative skill uniting college coaches and ad agency leaders. Without talent—the right talent—your chances of winning dwindle.

My boss, George Blaney, as you will continue to learn, is a special man. He had the demeanor of a priest. While he never drank or smoked, he was a true addict of the game of basketball. When I worked for him, he was the President of the National Association of Basketball Coaches (NABC). Our offices were ground zero for the basketball coaching community, which is every bit as tight-knit and insular as the creative ad agency community.

While I already knew so many big-time coaches from my playing career; working for Coach Blaney expanded my coaching relationships to new heights:

Jim Calhoun—UConn
Dave Gavitt—Big East Commissioner
Larry Brown—Kansas
Gary Williams—Boston College
Tom Penders—Fordham
Joe Mullaney- Providence
Pete Carrill—Princeton

Living five years in Worcester is like living ten years any-where else. It's the coldest place on earth, both literally and figuratively. We'd get snow in May. There was one good advan-tage to living in Worcester—it was 40 miles from Boston.

It was the mid-1980s and Larry Bird's Celtics ruled. We had tickets to all the legendary Lakers/Celtics championship series games. Magic vs. Bird, Showtime. Fellow Holy Cross assistant Eddie Reilly and I went to all of those games togeth-er in the old Boston Garden. Boy, was I lucky to witness the Golden Age of the NBA in person and with good seats.

Worcester was also thirty years from Boston culturally.

I became a little bored with basketball. Being on the road constantly wore me down. My hands used to get clammy be-fore every game, ever since Sacred Heart. They became drier and drier. The thrill was almost gone.

I got married and we had a son, Michael Thomas (he is a world-class copywriter and creative director today). I started to feel like it might be time to leave the world of basketball.

Just to get out of the cold and back to North Carolina, I took a job as an assistant at Western Carolina University near Asheville, NC. It was an abysmal job at a terrible school work-ing for a head coach who was about as different from George Blaney as one could be. It was like going from Father Flana-gan in *Boys' Town* to Jordan Belfort in *The Wolf of Wall Street*. It lasted one year. I no longer loved being part of the game of basketball. So I was looking to get out and do something where I could use my mind and my creativity.

Gaels blow out Louisville

Continued from back page

important thing was that we got the jump on them and were able to play our kind of game. We never got into a transition game with them; there's no way we could have won if we had tried to run up and down with them."

The Gaels scored the game's first eight points and opened a 22-12 lead at 11:11 of the first half on a Hamilton drive. But, typically, they allowed their foe to get back in the game. Griffith (32 points) led the way, and the Cardinals held a 28-27 lead with just under five minutes left in the first half.

"I think we kinda tired, from all the emotion we played with," Valvano said. "It took a toll on us."

QUICK BURST

But the Gaels, who led 39-36 at intermission, got out quickly in the second half, opening a 55-44 lead with Ruland seemingly pulling down every rebound. The closest the Cardinals were able to get was 61-54 with 7:43 left.

"Our press never hurt them, the first time this season it hasn't been effective; they handle it very well," Griffith said. "And if our press isn't working, we can't get into a transition-type game where we can get some easy baskets."

Griffith then added, "We just didn't have anybody who could handle Ruland," he said.

Former Mount Vernon standout, 6-8 Rodney Mc-Cray, tried, but he fouled out (with six points) with 5:08 to play.

"I might have (controlled

Iona coach Jim Valvano's hugs Mike Palma while assistant coach Dave Brown leads the cheers, after the Gaels' stunning upset last night in the Garden.

Post Photo by Nury Hernandez

Valvano embraces Palma after defeating Louisville in a packed
Madison Square Garden in 1980.

PAUL CAPPELLI

While I was at Iona in the late 1970s, I became great friends with a guy named Paul Cappelli. He was also an English major. We were in creative writing classes together and read each other's short stories, poems, articles, and scripts. We critiqued each other's work. We cared about each other's writing.

It was my first literary connection with a peer since the one I had with Rob Conroy in high school. I had some great teachers and mentors, most notably Emily Wilson in the English Department at Wake Forest University, who was one of the first people to encourage my writing. But Paul was special in that he was a peer and we were experiencing the creative rites of passage together.

When he graduated from Iona, he went to the School of Visual Arts in New York City to enter the world of advertising as a copywriter. His first job was at Ally & Gargano. Then he went to BBDO and wrote Pepsi commercials for Michael Jackson, including the one where his hair caught fire. Then Paul moved up to McCann-Erickson where he conceived the "Max Headroom" ads for Coca-Cola.

Almost every time I was in New York during my five years at Holy Cross (and that was a LOT), I'd get together with Paul for lunch or dinner or drinks. We grew even closer over the years. He'd invite me to visit whatever agency he was working for at the time. So I got into the offices of Ally & Gargano, BBDO, and McCann-Erickson *in their heydays*.

Through Paul, I got to know the ad business a little bit . He showed me his scripts and storyboards and I previewed his print ads. He asked my opinion of his work and trusted my feedback. I learned what great creative work really was through my friendship with him, as an outsider to the industry. An outsider on the verge of becoming a deep insider.

Leaving Basketball

In the spring of 1989, I met Paul for dinner at Guido's Restaurant, located in the back half of the Supreme Macaroni Pasta Store on 511 Ninth Avenue between 38th and 39th Streets (now demolished). It was the location for the black-and-white, back cover photo shoot for Billy Joel's album, *The Stranger*.

I told him it was time for me to get out of basketball and enter the advertising industry. He said he would hire me as an entry-level copywriter contingent on my also enrolling in night classes at SVA (School of Visual Arts). He offered me an annual salary of $24,000.

That dough was going to be difficult for my new family to live on, especially living in New York City. And no free Nikes! It would have been a great job for me if I were still single. And I think I would have had a great career as an advertising copywriter. But that wasn't my calling.

Paul could see the financial dilemma on my face. He knew me as well as anyone. The next words out of his mouth were maybe the most important ever spoken to me:

"I can't pay you more than $24,000 as an entry-level hire. We're a publicly-owned company. We have budgets set in stone. But, if you need to make more money, you're a great recruiter—why don't you be a headhunter and recruit copywriters and creative directors for agencies. You'd be great at that."

There it was. The vision for my future. The Calling. I decided to do that right then and there. That was my scene from an Italian restaurant—the scene that would set the stage for a thirty-five-year and still-running career in the ad agency business.

I moved our family to Raleigh, North Carolina, and set up an advertising desk there at the regional office of the international Executive Search firm, Management Recruiters International. I worked on straight commission with a $600 per month draw against commissions. I started work there on September 5, 1989. I placed five agency creatives, including two creative directors by the end of the year. In the fourth quarter of 1989 I billed $154,000. Half of that was mine and half went to the Raleigh franchise of MRI. My commission was $77,000 for four months of work. That's three times what Cappelli offered me for a full year. And I had only just begun.

I built an advertising recruiting franchise within the Raleigh office named Creative Search. After record-setting years with the largest recruiting organization in the country, I was ready to do my own thing. In 1993, I bought out my non-compete from MRI for $25,000 in cash and founded Palma Creative Search. It was the best $25,000 I ever invested—an investment into my own desire and ambition.

Every morning, I cut out the *Wall Street Journal* and *New York Times* advertising columns, printed them out and placed them in binders. I studied the Red Book every night, memorizing which agencies had what accounts and who the key players at each agency were. I'm lucky to have a photographic memory; it compensates for my lack of intelligence.

Becoming a top producing headhunter was pretty much the same drill as becoming an All-American basketball player. Instead of shooting 500 shots per day, I stayed connected on the telephone building relationships and creating opportunities for eight hours a day. That's connected phone time for eight hours, not sitting by the phone for eight hours.

In 1989, there was no email, no Internet, no websites. The gigantic cellular bag phone was as high-tech as it got. The fax machine was new technology. It was all phone work. The persuasive human voice is the most powerful business tool of all. Always was and still is.

When I sent a candidate's advertising portfolio to an agency client back then, it was a big, honking black hard shell portfolio case. These things cost around $100 to FedEx to an agency. Every creative agency of note gave me their FedEx account number. Chiat/Day was my first famous client. I placed eight creative directors with them in one year, 1992.

GSD&M was next—similar results. Then Crispin & Porter. Then EarlePalmerBrown. And before long, I had a reputation as a creative recruiter.

My goal was to send out five portfolios per day. I called those "sendouts." Another goal was to arrange five in-person interviews per week. I wouldn't go to lunch until I got a new job to fill—a fresh "job order"—every day. No new job, no food. It's one thing to say you're hungry for business, it's another to literally skip meals for new placements.

It's a cliche to say "hard work pays off" and credit the lessons I learned from my life in basketball for my advertising success. But it's much more complicated than that. It's setting the right goals, sticking to a routine, being disciplined to always stay in the present, maintaining an unwavering faith in yourself, trusting your skills, knowing when to let the game come to you, and when to initiate the action. It took a lot of perseverance. And a lot of luck. Everyone wants to succeed, but those who do, prepare for it and then stick with the plan.

If I had known how hard it would be and how lucky I would have to get to be successful in the advertising industry, I never would have tried it.

Learning From Legends

MY INTRODUCTION
TO RECRUITING

I learned the art of recruiting from being recruited by:

Stu Aberdeen—Tennessee
John Bach—Penn State
George Blaney—Holy Cross
Jim Boeheim—Syracuse
Lou Carnesecca—St. John's
Bobby Cremins—South Carolina
Chuck Daly—Penn
Eddie Fogler—North Carolina
Bill Foster—Duke
Dave Gavitt—Providence

John Kresse—St. John's
John Lotz—Florida
Neill McGeachy—Wake Forest
Frank McGuire—South Carolina
Rick Pitino—Hawaii
Bill Raftery—Seton Hall
Fred Schaus—Purdue
Dean Smith—North Carolina
Bill Stein—Georgetown
John Thompson—Georgetown
Dick Vitale—Detroit
Bob Wenzel—Duke

I also learned from these coaches by working with them at the Five-Star Camp:

John Calipari—UMass, Memphis, Kentucky, Arkansas
PJ Carlesimo—Seton Hall, Golden State Warriors
Pete Carrill—Princeton
Seth Greenberg—Virginia Tech, ESPN
Bob Hurley, Sr.—St. Anthony's HS
Brendan Malone—multiple NBA coaching jobs
Tom Penders—Fordham, Texas
Rick Pitino—BU, Providence, New York Knicks, Kentucky,
    Boston Celtics, Louisville, Iona, St. John's

Jim Boeheim

SYRACUSE

To give you an idea how old I am, when Jim Boeheim recruited me, he was still an assistant coach at Syracuse, not yet the head coach. For those keeping score, Boeheim recently retired in 2023 after leading the Orange for forty-seven seasons. That's old! He was a hard-working basketball nerd. He was also a pretty good college player who played in the Eastern League, which was then a "minor league" for the NBA. He brought some playing cred into our home when he arrived at our front door.

First off, if you got to our front door for a home visit, you were indeed a hard worker. Frank Morris hated that I was heavily recruited and did little to facilitate the recruiting process for these college coaches. In fact, he discouraged it.

He probably thought it would go to my head (it did anyway). He never once set up a meeting between any coach and me. Every couple of weeks, Mr. Morris called me to his little office in the gym and handed me thirty or forty letters from colleges. No advice. No counsel. No questions about what I was doing—whether I had any visits planned. He never talked about colleges with me. I was on my own.

So if you got to my door, you had to work extra hard and call our home directly at 516-379-3093. Boeheim did. And Syracuse had a great track record recruiting Long Island going back to Jimmy Brown at Manhasset High School. My mom made him coffee and served cookies, as she did for every coach who visited our home. I'm lucky to have such a great mom.

Boeheim and I talked about basketball more than we focused on Syracuse. We went back and forth on shooting and out-of-bounds plays and how to beat the zone defense (funny how he became famous for Syracuse's vaunted 2-3 zone).

Boeheim told me what he liked about my game and what he thought I could do better. He had attended our recent game against Chaminade High School and I could tell he watched closely and had a photographic memory. He was equally complimentary and constructively critical. I think great recruiters do that. They're low-key without patronizing you or blowing smoke up your ass. But they still know how to make you feel good.

He did say in his cerebral way, "I don't think I've seen a small forward do as many things as well as you did the other night this entire season. We knew you were a great shooter, but you do a lot more than shoot. You pass well and you rebound well. You have great hands. You don't turn it over." I thought that was pretty cool to hear all that in Boeheim's deadpan way. I liked him and respected him.

There were two problems.

He never stopped talking. My parents actually said goodnight and went up to bed about 10 p.m. while we continued on about basketball.

There was no Big East Conference yet—another sign of how old I am. I would have to battle those Syracuse winters with no Big East, no ESPN, and no Carrier Dome.

I wasn't interested in going to Syracuse to play in Manley Fieldhouse and eventually Jim Boehem had to tell his boss Roy Danforth that. When I told him I wasn't going to take a campus visit—he asked me where I wanted to go. I told him "probably Duke," to which he said "that's a great choice for the way you play, you would fit in well with Coach Foster's system." And I'm thinking to myself, "Fit in? I'm gonna average 28 as a freshman."

I had swagger back then, but not the humble.

Three business takeaways from JIM BOEHEIM

1. Be astute about your target. Understand their skills, what they do well and what they need to do to get better. Top

talent and new business prospects want to get better. They want to reach their potential. Help them do that.

2. Don't BS and patronize your target with hyperbole.

3. Don't overstay your welcome. Know when it's time to go home.

Lou Carnesecca

ST. JOHN'S

I first met Coach Carnesecca at Sacred Heart School in seventh grade at a Catholic Youth Organization communion breakfast. He was like an Italian leprechaun, such a jolly and jovial man. He loved basketball and he loved St. John's, the only major college basketball program in the New York City area when I was a kid. That's where Frankie Alagia went to play. And Frankie had a really good four years there.

After that communion breakfast, my first coach Jack Johnston asked Louie if he could bring our team to a St. John's practice in Jamaica, Queens. So about a week later, there I was in Alumni Hall at my first college basketball practice. I was blown away at how good these guys were! But even at eleven years old, I could see myself out there someday.

When Coach Carnesecca came to our home in 1975, it was an extra special night. It was nothing like the charisma-lacking visit from Boeheim. It was more like the pope was coming over. My mom broke out her best coffee cups along with Italian pastries, not cookies. My dad wore a nice shirt. We were like royalty. Assistant Coach John Kresse was with Carnesecca and he was a class act himself. Ironically, Kresse later recruited one of my best players at Bishop McGuinness when he was head coach at College of Charleston.

Louie's big recruiting pitch was comparing me to Rick Barry, whom he coached during his brief stint with the New York Nets of the American Basketball Association when they played in Commack, Long Island. Sure enough, a week later, Coach Carnesecca told the *New York Daily News* that they really wanted to sign Mike Palma of St. Agnes because he's "the next Rick Barry." There it was in the newspaper. Heck, I believed him. I was gonna average 28 as a freshman for the Red Storm and wear number 24.

There were two problems.

I wasn't Rick Barry, I was barely 6-5.

There was no Big East Conference yet. There were no dormitories and no "campus life" to speak of. It was a commuter campus. I felt like I wanted that experience. I wanted to play in the ACC, the best conference on the East Coast. It's hard to believe I spurned St. John's and Coach Carnesecca not once, but twice. If my dad hadn't made a sales call to Seaford High

School, I probably would have played for Louie when I transferred back home.

I can't tell you how many times I used the "Rick Barry ploy" when recruiting creative folks: "If you seize this opportunity, you can be the next David Lubars." Or Bob Barrie. Or whoever was hot in the One Show Annual that year. It's quite a seductive tactic.

Three business takeaways from LOU CARNESSECCA

1. Be lovable, memorable, and unforgettable.

2. Flatter your target with realistic aspiration.

3. If you're going to be a character, make sure you have character.

Bonus: Pursue Italian-American talent. It's easier for an Italian-American to sell another. It just is. It's "this Sicilian thing, Michael that's been going on for two thousand years."

Bobby Cremins
SOUTH CAROLINA

When Bobby Cremins recruited me, he was Frank Mc-Guire's assistant at South Carolina. He had traces of brown hair, but he was still prematurely gray. He attended a lot of my games, especially the bigger ones played at Hofstra. Play-off games and big-draw games. He was at my best games and he happened to be at my worst game.

We played Jack Curran's Archbishop Molloy team in their gym in December 1974. Why Frank Morris ever agreed to do that was always beyond me. When we played our "home" game against Molloy, it was at St. John's or Hofstra. In their gym, with Curran's refs, we were dead. I had three fouls in four minutes. In the second half, Curran triple-teamed me. I wound up with five points. As I walked out of the gym after the game, there was Coach Cremins. He said, "Don't worry Mike, we still want you." I couldn't believe anyone would still want me after scoring five points, but that felt really good to hear.

South Carolina's recruiting style was memorable. On Mother's Day, a beautiful bouquet of flowers was delivered to our home with a note to Mrs. Palma from Coach Frank McGuire. Then the same on Thanksgiving. And then again on Christmas. And then finally again on Easter. It was so charming.

So when I send a candidate or a new business prospect a thoughtful gift, it reminds me of Cremins and South Carolina. The Palma Group sends out many gifts to our clients and prospects. That's a big part of an effective business development system. There's no substitute for a thoughtful gift.

There were two problems.

I never actually met Frank McGuire. He attended the LI Catholic HS Championship game at Hofstra my junior season in 1974. Or, so I was told. We lost to St. Anthony's, which was no great sin. They were pretty good. I went for 31 points and 18 rebounds in a low-scoring game (any game not in the 80 point range was low-scoring for St. Agnes).

We were up at halftime but they came out in the second half and double-teamed me. Mr. Morris, in his characteristic stubbornness, refused to call a timeout when they made their run. Then after the game, he sent the message to Coach McGuire outside the locker room that I was "too upset" to talk to him. The truth is I didn't even know he was there until my mother told me she talked to him after the game for fifteen minutes.

South Carolina dropped out of the ACC in 1974 and became an independent.

Cremins was named Head Coach at Appalachian State in 1975. And we played them in Winston-Salem my freshman year. After the season, Bruce Springsteen booked a show at Appalachian State in Boone, N.C. on the *Born to Run* tour and I called Coach Cremins to to see if he'd be around. He said he was going to be out of town recruiting but he insisted that I stay at his condo. He left me the keys under the mat and a great note with all the instructions for the house. That's the kind of guy he is.

Three business takeaways from BOBBY CREMINS

1. Be empathetic after a loss. Use a loss as a renewed commitment. You can't Walk with a Humble Swagger without empathy.

2. Send thoughtful gifts to prospects and targets. Not self-promotional items—but things of real value.

3. Mi casa es su casa. Be a friend.

John Thompson

GEORGETOWN

The first time I ever flew on an airplane was my official visit to Georgetown in September of my senior year in 1974. I remember my dad driving me to the old Eastern Airlines Terminal at LaGuardia Airport and flying the "shuttle" to Washington, DC. Georgetown was such a perfect school for me. I loved the campus and I felt like I really fit with the student body: a bunch of Northeast Catholic school kids.

When I walked into Coach Thompson's office to meet him, there was the now-famous deflated basketball on his desk. It was there to signify the insignificance of a playing career when it is over. It was an obvious metaphor, but effective. I would have gone to Georgetown if I didn't play basketball. But, I doubt they would have me if I couldn't shoot. And therein lies the irony of the deflated basketball on the desk. Hey, thanks for the sage advice, but we all know why you want me here. I do remember feeling slightly uncomfortable in Coach Thompson's office because he didn't look me in the eye when he spoke.

Coach Thompson was in his second season and the program was still in its very formative stages. It would have taken a real leap of faith for me to commit to Georgetown in the spring of 1975. But I loved the guy who recruited me, an assistant named Bill Stein. He was a great recruiter. He felt like a good friend. He called me all the time and wrote me at least one handwritten letter every week.

So whenever I wrote a handwritten note to a recruit as a coach or advertising recruiter, I called it a "Bill Stein." Such a nice, caring, classy touch.

Coach Thompson, Bill Stein and academic coach Mary Fenlon came to one of my games at Hofstra during my senior season at St. Agnes. Afterward, we all went to the Apollo Diner in East Meadow and ate cheeseburgers with my parents and sisters. Coach Thompson had a vanilla milkshake for dessert.

There were two problems.

Georgetown was still not very good. It was very early in Thompson's tenure.

If there were a Big East Conference in 1975, I might have taken the risk and signed with Georgetown. A recurring theme here...

Ironically, Coach Thompson's team ended my playing career in the Sweet 16 round of the NCAA Tournament in 1980 when Iona lost to Sleepy Floyd's team by three points in the Providence Civic Center. Damn deflated basketball metaphor. It came back to haunt me.

Three business takeaways from JOHN THOMPSON

1. Stay focused on the Long Game. Use your advertising career as a means to an end.

2. Write handwritten notes—"love letters" to your prospects. Recruiting is a courtship.

3. Always look your recruits in the eye.

Chuck Daly

PENN

A week or so after that first plane flight, I took an Amtrak train down to the 30th Street Station in Philadelphia to visit the University of Pennsylvania, coached by then-relatively unknown Chuck Daly. (Daly of course went on to win consecutive NBA titles leading the "Bad Boy" Detroit Pistons in 1989 and 1990). Not much went well. I waited at the station to be picked up for over an hour. I didn't like the way the city smelled. Hard to explain, but it smelled completely different than New York. The dorm rooms were small. Among the students I talked with, nobody seemed to care about the basketball team.

I played a pickup game in The Palestra, (Penn's historic home gym which was built in 1927), with some of the players. They were REALLY good. The names aren't famous, but they had the best players of any school I visited: Ron Haigler, Bob Bigelow, Henry Johnson, Mark Lonetto, and John Engles. I actually couldn't see myself getting big minutes on a team with so many great players.

However, Coach Daly was a great recruiter. Somehow, he got me admitted to Penn as a student. *That* alone takes a great recruiter, but he also made me feel that he could help me become an NBA player through player development. He actually worked with me during my visit to the Palestra. He was very hands on and he cared about his players, who all loved him like a father.

Within two years, he was in the NBA and none of his players were (except Bigelow, who wasn't even the best player on the Penn team).

The best lesson I learned from Daly that applied to my advertising career was how well-dressed he was and how that made such a strong first impression. It seems superficial, but never underestimate the effect of a well-attired professional. It's not about how rich or fancy you are—it's about taste. There's no substitute for great taste. It says so much. That's who Chuck Daly was; he dressed the way he built his program and his professional teams—impeccably. Thoughtfully conceived with attention to detail.

There were two problems.

They left me waiting at the station to smell the foulness of Philadelphia.

They were in the Ivy League and I would have had to do

work-study for financial aid on top of the enormous time commitment of playing basketball.

Three business takeaways from CHUCK DALY

1. Look sharp. You only have one chance at a first impression.

2. Be sharp. Be on time. Be prompt. Waiting at the train station for an hour for someone to pick me up kind of pissed me off.

3. Be committed to the goals and success of your client.

Dick Vitale

DETROIT

Dickie V breezed into our living room midsummer between my junior and senior years at St. Agnes. This guy was a piece of work! What a great salesman! There was no doubt this guy was going to make the University of Detroit a successful Div. I program. I have never been around anyone with his infectious enthusiasm. If Jim Boeheim was deadpan Bob Newhart, Vitale was Dom DeLuise. He was hysterical. My family loved him.

Dickie V taught me the power of positive energy. The Dick Vitale we saw on ESPN was the same guy in my living room in 1974—same jargon, same Vitale-isms. He was always "on." He drank his coffee black, but he really didn't need it. He was caffeine personified. If you can get high-school All-Americans to consider attending the University of Detroit, you have unwavering faith and gusto. While Vitale was a great recruiter, he was also a great defensive tactician—not surprising because so much of defense success requires motivation and desire more than specific skills.

I never took a visit to Detroit. But, as you would imagine, NOBODY recruited me with more energy and passion. He was good friends with Howard Garfinkel who co-owned the only scouting service available to college coaches those days. It was called HSBI, short for *High School Basketball Illustrated*. When "Garf" and his partner, the saintly Tom Konchalski rated me a five-star prospect after my junior season, the floodgates opened for guys in the Midwest who had never seen me play. Vitale, Freddy Schaus (Purdue), Lute Olson (Iowa), John Bach (Penn State) all descended upon Rockville Centre, Long Island to recruit the Palma family in the summer of 1974.

Much of the attention I received was due to Garfinkel's and Konchalski's scouting assessment that I was the "next Jerry Sloan." But, it was Vitale who was persistent enough to get into our living room.

Persistence is the single most important trait I learned from Vitale and I took it into my career in advertising. It sounds trite, but it takes guts to recruit top talent. It takes guts to pick up the phone. It takes the ability to overcome rejection and objections. Vitale couldn't care less if he was at Detroit or on the moon—he had a great opportunity and he was going to try and sell you on it. That's what great recruiters do.

There were two problems.

I wasn't moving to Michigan. It was like going to the frozen tundra of Lambeau Field in Green Bay in my young mind.

I was not a great defensive player and Vitale was a defensive coach who loved low-scoring games. I was run and gun. I was a volume shooter.

Three business takeaways from DICK VITALE

1. Have energy and enthusiasm first, then focus on the task second.

2. Be persistent and your dreams will come true.

3. Study the industry periodicals and reports. Know the field.

Rick Pitino

HAWAII

Rick Pitino just showed up on our front porch and rang the doorbell. My mom answered the door and asked him who he was. He said he was a friend of mine, looking not much older than me. I did know Rick from the All-American Basketball Camp in Smithtown, N.Y. He was a counselor when I was a thirteen-year-old camper from Sacred Heart Elementary School. But, I wouldn't have called him a "friend." He was actually more of a role model—nicknamed "Rick the Rifle" from nearby St. Dom's HS. He was five years older than me. Really competitive guy.

My mom said, "Let me go get Michael." However, she didn't invite him in as she was unsure who he was—she knew all my friends. He added, "Please tell Mike I'm now the assistant basketball coach at the University of Hawaii."

She says, "Okay, do you have an appointment? He didn't tell me you were coming. If I knew, I would have made you coffee and cookies."

Pitino says, "No, I didn't have an appointment. But I was in the neighborhood."

My mom comes to my room and asks, "Do you know a guy named Rick Pitino? He's at the door and says he's your friend."

I wasn't ever going to the University of Hawaii. I had never even flown on an airplane before. And I think Pitino knew if he called to make an appointment, he never would have even gotten the chance to make his pitch. So he rolled the dice and got in. That's what great recruiters do. That's what great ad agency and business development people do—they make sure they get a chance to pitch. They get their foot in the door. If they go down, they go down in flames.

I learned this great lesson from Rick: be polite and professional but make sure you get your foot in the door.

Within minutes, he offered me a full scholarship right on the spot. He said it would be the biggest news in the history of Hawaii basketball if I signed. I honestly didn't even know where Hawaii was. I had to go into my room and look at a globe.

The funny thing is that Pitino wound up signing two *great* Long Island players in Reggie Carter of Lutheran and Henry Hollingsworth of Freeport. So a lot of success is simply showing up.

One of the first ways I ever got a new business meeting for an agency was to tell the prospect that we were "going to be in their neighborhood" on a particular date. It worked more than occasionally. That's what else I got from Pitino—show up and be in the neighborhood.

Years later, as a college coach when I worked the Five Star Camp in the Pocono Mountains with him, he kind of took me under his wing. He gave me pointers on recruiting habits—how to establish a routine, creating a plan, and then fanatically sticking to it. I definitely applied a disciplined routine to my recruiting days when establishing and growing The Palma Group.

Pitino stressed the importance of outworking the competition. He personified the "early bird gets the worm" theory. Nobody is born a great coach, but you will and work your way there. Rick was that guy. He believed he was special and it became a self-fulfilling prophecy.

There were two problems.

While I wanted to leave home for a better climate, Honolulu was geographically a little ridiculous.

Hawaii Basketball had no history, no tradition. I didn't even know what league they were in—but I knew it wasn't the ACC.

Three business takeaways from RICK PITINO

1. If you're gonna go down, go down in flames.

2. Get in the room. Get in the pitch. Get in front of your target.

3. You really can outwork the competition if you fanatically adhere to a disciplined plan and program for improvement. Excellence is achieved one painstaking day at a time.

George Blaney

HOLY CROSS

Holy Cross was once the gold standard of college basket-ball in the Northeast. The Crusaders' storied history includ-ed both NCAA and NIT championships. Bob Cousy, then the greatest point guard of all time, played there. There was no Big East, but at the time Holy Cross, St. John's, Providence and Syracuse were the preeminent college basketball pro-grams in the Northeast. Holy Cross was a natural contender for my basketball services. Heck, even my first idol, Lew Al-cindor visited Holy Cross as a high school senior.

George Blaney didn't act humble—he actually was hum-ble. It was no fake humility that you often see from a lot of basketball (and advertising) guys. When he walked into our home, he was sincere, soft-spoken and polite. You could just tell he was a genuinely good and moral man. You would never know from his demeanor that he played in the NBA for the New York Knicks in the early 1960s.

Blaney was a lot like Boeheim actually: serious, low-key, and logical in his approach. But there was also a riveting intensity in his eyes at the same time. He and his assistant attended many St. Agnes games.

Coach Blaney's biggest differentiator from the other college coaches was the way he stressed the value of a Holy Cross degree, particularly in New York and Boston. He emphasized how special a Jesuit Liberal Arts education is. Even the University of Pennsylvania of the Ivy League didn't stress the true benefit of a college basketball scholarship at their esteemed institution. Blaney was the first coach in our home to talk about academics in a meaningful way.

I drove up to Holy Cross with my dad for a campus visit. Like Georgetown, it was a good fit and it came without the risk of an upstart losing team, which the Hoyas were at the time. Holy Cross' players were good—really good. Looking back, I think everyone there, the players and the staff, liked my dad more than me—with my insufferable ego and all. Years later, my good friend Joe Carballeira, who was a point guard on the '75 Crusaders, confirmed that suspicion.

As you have already read, I wound up working for George Blaney at The Cross for five years as his lead recruiter assistant coach. As a result, George actually had a greater effect on my adult life than Jim Valvano did. In many ways, he became more of a mentor and a role model. To this day, I consider what Coach Blaney might think when making an important decision.

One great lesson he taught me was "never let your boss beat you to the office." Boy, was that smart advice. He also taught me to trust my brain. He knew I was intelligent, despite some of the dumbass things I did. He gave me emotional and intellectual confidence, which I never really had as a kid.

If anyone in my life ever walked with a humble swagger, it was George Blaney. He taught me it was ok to have the swagger, but the humble part has to be learned. You have to get knocked down a few times. Defeat triggers humility. You have to be grateful for your luck. Gratitude is the foundation for humility.

As a high school player, he taught me it was ok to think you're a great player. He knew I would have to get twenty shots a game to be happy. And he was fine with that. He knew how much courage it took to shoot the third shot after missing two in a row. He looked me in the eye and said, "What I love most about you is your confidence. You never think you're gonna miss a shot."

I really thought hard about going to Holy Cross. I felt comfortable that Coach Blaney would be great to play for and that I would get a great degree with real-world value.

Again, there were two problems.

Worcester was the coldest place west of Siberia.

There was no Big East in 1975. A lot of people don't know

this, but Holy Cross was a charter invitee to the Big East in 1979. That year, the core of the Big East was formed by Dave Gavitt when Providence College, St. John's, Georgetown and Syracuse invited Seton Hall, UConn, Holy Cross, Rutgers and Boston College. Holy Cross turned down the invitation, as did Rutgers initially; while BC, Seton Hall and UConn accepted. Villanova and Pittsburgh joined shortly thereafter.

Three business takeaways from GEORGE BLANEY

1. Be a gentleman—always.

2. Have integrity.

3. Sell the true benefit to understand the real opportunity.

Jim Valvano

IONA

As you might imagine by now, Coach Valvano abruptly changed the course of my life (if not, you haven't been reading very carefully and I'll share the blame for that). But, it was so much more than my basketball life. He was the first coach I played for who actually cared about my development as a student, as a writer, and as a young man. He was not just my coach, mentor, and teacher but he was also a friend who felt like he was part of my family.

I remember when our team returned to LaGuardia Airport from the very first Great Alaska Shootout in November, 1979 (it was also the first basketball game ever televised by ESPN), and Coach V grabbed me at baggage claim. It was very late at night after an eight-hour flight after a really tough two-point loss to Kentucky in the championship game.

He said, "Michael, your father is in the hospital. He had a heart attack when we were in Alaska, but he didn't want you to worry. We have a cab ready to take you home to Long Island. He's going to be okay." I immediately thought back to the time my dad saved Mr. McCann's life at my sixth-grade basketball practice. I hugged Coach V and took a cab home to Long Island. That was the way my last season as a basketball player began.

On that note, now is a good time to make the stylistic transition from prose to "blog post." The following format is consistent throughout the rest of this book. What follows is the best of mikepalma.com.

Seven Lessons learned from JIM VALVANO
Relevant to the agency business and life

Jim Valvano—he's become synonymous with the word *underdog*. In our two seasons together, we went 52-10, won two ECAC championships and made it to the NCAA Tournament both years. We beat the Kansas Jayhawks, Pittsburgh, St. John's, Wichita State, Seton Hall and Mike Krzyzewski's Army squad thrice.

We also beat the eventual tournament champion, Louisville, 77-60 in Madison Square Garden in February of 1980. They were nicknamed the "Doctors of Dunk." We were a bunch of tough New York kids without a nickname. That season, we ranked in the top 20 of the final AP poll.

Playing for V was an emotional roller coaster—such incredible highs and lows. There was no "normal." Everything he did was a challenge to our manhood and our competitiveness. He thrived on adversity.

He and I had an unusual bond—we were both English majors and literary students. We often discussed the frailty of the human condition and the duty of the writer to make language new.

I learned seven key lessons from Jimmy that apply not just to basketball, but to the agency business and life:

1. *The only two things that are real in this world are Achievements and Relationships.* V would finish this thought with, "and we get to have both." Forty years later, this theory has withstood the test of time. Everything else just fades away, like cheap ink.

2. *Never accept in victory what you wouldn't in defeat.* Boy, does this apply to the pitch process. You might get away with less than your best occasionally; but it will surely come back to haunt you when you need it most.

3. *Dare to Dream.* As usual, V usually had a subtitle to his headlines. For this one it was, "and then out-dream yourself." Our dream was to beat the nation's No. 1 team in the country in the 9 o'clock game at The Garden.

What's your team's dream? Agency of the Year? What's your personal dream? Marketer of the Year? A One Show Pencil? Go do it...anything is possible if you plan for it.

4. *Always know the time and score.* Sounds simple, right? It's not. Your shelf life as a professional has an expiration date. And your value is measured in wins. Never lose sight of the clock and scoreboard. LinkedIn is littered with expert losers.

5. *Success requires a system.* All great coaches have a system. The system wins and the system loses. The players are just executing the system. Great players in a bad system often lose. And good ones in a great system almost always win.

6. *Basketball is a cumulative game.* Life is a cumulative game; so is your career, your agency or your brand—it's *all* a cumulative game. It all counts—not just the last two minutes. A missed opportunity is a missed opportunity.

7. *Make enthusiasm a habit.* Our industry attracts cynics... don't be one. Train your enthusiasm, don't curb it. Foster it. Develop it. Seek inspiration. Find and channel your inner Coach V, I did.

Recruiting

GETTING TOP TALENT
AT YOUR AGENCY

1

FINDING MAGIC: 10 TIPS FOR RECRUITING TOP TALENT

The most valuable capital in the communications industry is superstar talent. Despite the fact that we've done our best to commoditize it, talent remains the heaviest currency. Read the trades, the biggest stories have been the comings and goings of agency linchpins (unless media itself is a big story). There are always new account wins and losses; but the daily dish is always a big name coming in or moving on. We're an industry of high-profile peripateticism.

Why? Because what's at the top filters down. Recruiting key senior management talent is the most expeditious, and often the most effective way to upgrade an agency. Attracting a star, or better yet, a rising star is often what separates a good agency from a great agency.

So, what is a superstar? There are two kinds—let's call them Pistol and Magic.

Pistol is Pete Maravich—all-time NCAA scorer (three years, no three point line). Rock star. Degree-of-difficulty champion. Not a winner. *Does not make anyone around him better.* Loses. Pouts when not the center of attention. Is a character.

Magic is Magic Johnson—Rejects personal achievement. *Makes anyone around him better.* Wins. Makes it look easy. Always positive. Just wins. Has character (maybe not self-restraint, but character).

Hey, I loved Pistol Pete. I idolized him. But, I was twelve years old and didn't know any better. He could have been on the cover of *Tiger Beat*. And I hated Earvin Johnson—I was a Celtics fan living near Boston in the 80's. I wanted to wipe that smile right off his face. But, I realize now the difference between the two superstars: one made everyone around him better. The other didn't. Suffice it to say, when seeking top talent—look for Magic.

Okay, we're talking about an impact hire—talent that will excite clients, prospects and employees: A Creative Director, Account Director, Media Director or potential partner. Here are some guidelines that might help you evaluate and attract this type of talent:

1. *Don't* be overly influenced by geography. It's tempting to think that the ideal candidate (or their spouse) may have personal ties to your state or region. They may, or they may not. They will only move for one reason: Opportunity. Geography is a reason people DON'T move. It is rarely the reason they do. And if it is, it's not a good enough reason. Geography, compensation, titles, etc. are secondary, supporting factors. Opportunity is the primary factor.

2. *Don't* screen candidates based on the size of their current agency. It's also tempting to assume that the best fit will come from a similarly sized current environment. This is an *idea* business. No two agencies are the same anyway, regardless of size. Sometimes mid-sized agencies are intimidated by candidates from multinational companies, and larger agencies are sometimes prone to frowning upon candidates from smaller shops.

3. *Don't* screen candidates primarily on category experience. You strive to increase differentiation for your clients—so consider taking this opportunity to do the same for your agency. Category experience is negligible compared to talent.

4. *Don't* overlook the spec. The superstar's portfolio/reel/ work is chock full of visible, award-winning work—but, some of their best work was never produced. They love to talk about this stuff, and it will also provide an interesting peek

into their potential. Don't diminish a great idea just because it didn't sell.

5. *Do* throw out the checklists and spreadsheets. This is a high-stakes creative hire, not an engineer. Trust your eyes, your ears and your instincts.

6. *Do* determine exactly what you need. What do you need for your candidate to accomplish? Can they? Don't recruit top talent to do a job they can't do. Or they can do it, but you won't let them. Consider the obstacles to accomplishing your needs.

7. *Do* notice and study the work you admire. Look for campaigns that are smart, creative and relevant to your business. Don't under OR overestimate the major award shows. Trust your eyes.

8. *Do* initiate a conversation. Spend time on the phone with your candidates and you'll get an initial sense of chemistry and interest. Emails, tweets, etc. are fine—but dialogue is a stronger recruiting/evaluation tool. Ask them questions. Ask them what their principles are. Ask them what they know about your agency. Address their perceptions.

9. *Do* study the case studies. Ask the candidate to present a couple of their most interesting case studies—the two they're most proud of. Ask them to take you through the campaigns—from

strategy to results. This is separate from their portfolio work.

10. *Do* stress your agency's and your personal values. Don't assume everyone has the same methods, tactics or endgame.

2

HOW TO RETAIN TOP TALENT: FIVE TIPS

Doesn't it seem that our world has become one big talent show? Turn on the TV (painful, I know)...*The Voice, Dancing With the Stars, American Idol, X Factor, You're a Star, The Glee Project, America's Got Talent* are just a handful of wannabe-celebrity talent shows. Or just log on to Facebook for daily videos of kids and cats performing stupid tricks. We can't escape the exhibitionist mentality so pervasive in today's society. In a winner-take-all world, everybody seems to want their 15 minutes of fame.

The creative advertising industry has its own version of talent shows...we call them Awards Shows. Cannes Lions, One Show Pencils, Effies and Addys have replaced the erstwhile Clios that crashed due to its inherent overindulgence of egomania. But, our industry has never been exempt from

"Hey look at me, I'm a star" syndrome. This is not a criticism but a commentary. My core business is delivering talent. Like the pizza man, I am part of the food chain, a ghost in this machine and my comments reflect thirty-five dreadful years of experience.

Creative agencies are purely the sum total of their collective talent base. Without talent, there is no point of differentiation. Without talent, there is no value proposition; just boring processes. It's funny how clients and search consultants insist on a certain critical mass of total employees yet they only want to pay for a few. But, that's another post. This one is about keeping the talent you have recruited intact.

Recognizing top talent is relatively easy. Identifying top talent is, as well. Recruiting the talent is tricky, but do-able. Delivering talent? Tough. Maximizing top talent? Very difficult. Retaining it—the toughest challenge of all. And if you lose it, it's wasted on YOU.

So how do you do it? Nobody asked me, but here are a few tips:

1. *Program the hire for success from the start.* Most unsuccessful hires can be traced to the early days of the employee's tenure. Do you have an onboarding process? An agency orientation? A mentor program? Everybody needs a mentor. Have you prepared your current employees for an impact hire? It amazes me when an agency hires top talent and the candidate shows up unannounced for their first

day of work. Or worse, when they have to supervise folks who have no idea who they are. Too often, an introductory email is sent out weeks following the hire and there is little definition of the candidate's role.

2. *The 100-day review.* When things break down, they break down fast. It's critical to conduct reviews early and often. Simple questions like, "how does the actual job compare to the job description?" And, "are you more excited or less excited about the opportunity than when you accepted the offer?" At 200 days, the questions become more personal and specific, "Are you challenged?" "Are you still having fun?"

3. *Everybody has an opinion.* On operational issues, on creative issues, on cultural issues, on social issues. When I ask an employed job seeker why they are looking to move, too often they say, "Nobody cares about my opinion, I'm just a hired gun." Or worse, if they're asked for their opinion—it isn't valued and they feel ignored. Seek opinions from top talent...constantly.

4. *Decisions, Decisions.* Nothing pisses off top talent more than evasive partners and colleagues that make passive-aggressive decisions. Or worse, are completely indecisive. Tomorrow never comes for them. They feel they are wasting their talent trying to catch jellyfish. Be decisive in defining roles. Dictatorship is okay as long as it's fair and benevolent.

5. *Promises, Promises.* In my experience, and that's more than 1,500 hires, it breaks down far more often on the agency side than the candidate side. It hurts me to say this, because the agencies are my clients (they pay everyone); but it never helps long-term to "sell" a candidate on an opportunity. If anything, underpromise and over-deliver. There's nothing worse than investing in top talent, introducing them to a key client and losing them because the reality of the opportunity differs from the perception.

3

SEVEN HABITS OF HIGHLY EFFECTIVE CREATIVE PEOPLE

Creative people think they defy convention. They believe they are anomalies—each one an intricate, complex web. They remind me of dungarees, a badge of non-conformity until everyone conforms to them. Most people in the communications industry think they are creative, except for the bean counters. Ironically, it is the controllers that have had to be the *most* creative people at the agency these days, especially when figuring out how to monetize their social and digital offerings.

The problem however, is that true creativity is on the wane. This is not exactly a watershed era for artists, writers, poets—not just ad men and women. Where's the work? Where's Mona Lisa? Who's our Beethoven? What's the new

Great American Novel? Who's the next Jack Kerouac? F. Scott Fitzgerald? Where's the great ad tagline of this century? And what in the hell has happened to rock and roll? Does it even exist? There are all kinds of theories about how and why. Nothing can be proven, but there has to be some inextricable link to technology. Does it make us use our minds (our creative minds) more or less? What will we call this creative generation? *The Googlers?* The *"I'm Feeling Lucky"* Age? Or maybe *Generation WTF.*

What I've found is that truly creative people tend to downplay their "creativity." And pseudo-creatives tend to overplay it and dramatize it. But this is not about attitudes or cerebral posturing. Intelligence is somewhat relative and subjective, anyway. Sometimes it seems the smarter you are, the dumber you really are. Columbo always cracked the case by asking the dumb questions. This is about habits—proactive habits. Things creative people DO, not think.

Of the many myths, the notion of "eccentricity" is most often assimilated with creativity. Creative people often have a peculiar trait or two, but no more so than the average schmuck that makes your sandwich for lunch. We just pay closer attention to the creative shamans and become smitten with their oddities. Another myth is that creative people are "deeper"—they're heavy—more sensitive to the human condition. At least I know that I'm shallow—an inch deep and a mile wide. A dilettante. I don't confuse my one great gift with intelligence or creativity. I'm blessed. Blessed with what?

I forgot. Oh yeah, I was born with a great memory (but, it's short). Fortunately, our world rewards a good, short memory.

These are some of the common denominators that I've observed in working with highly effective creative people:

1. *Painters paint.* Writers write. Designers design. Singers sing. The great Al Jolson, in his dying days, would stop people on the street and tell them he was Al Jolson. When folks didn't believe him—he would sing to them—right there on the street. True, today he would be diagnosed with dementia, but the illustration is that he *had* to sing. It was in his DNA. And when he could no longer sing, he died. Quickly. Effective creative people *create*. Constantly. They don't talk about it. They do it.

2. *Compulsive addiction to their craft.* I've noticed that the most effective creative people can't stop. They can't walk away from the table. And if they do, they come back shortly. They either stay up ridiculously late at night, or rise ridiculously early to create. They can't rest easily because their active, creative mind won't allow them. They do not think about getting better or improving. They just know that the more they do something, the better they will get. They create while on vacation. They wake up in the middle of the night and write ideas. They can't stop learning all they can about their craft.

3. *Unhurried.* Truly effective creative people are able to "slow the game down." They won't be rushed. They love what they do too much to rush it. They savor their craft like a foodie savors a meal. We sometimes confuse this *unhurriedness* for slowness, and we bellyache when deadlines aren't met. But effectiveness should not be confused with timeliness. In short, effective creative people are on their own schedule. And often in their own world. This is not "eccentricity"—it's the ability to recognize and adhere to a process. It's actually quite the opposite of "eccentricity."

4. *Purity of Heart.* The best creatives I've been fortunate to observe are purists. They reject and abhor anything that is impure or unnatural. They possess moral turpitude and a respect for the gods of their discipline. Their craft is sacrosanct. I play golf with my dentist. He's a great dentist, the best I've ever seen. When on the links, he wears two golf gloves, one on each hand. His hands are that important to him. Great creatives treat their mind the same way.

5. *Minimalism.* Great creatives travel lightly. They are not seduced by the treasures of this world. Their treasure is between their ears. They are otherworldly. They would do what they do for free if food, clothing, and energy were *gratis.* They see money as a necessary evil. If they collect anything at all, it's something associated with their craft. Objects almost embarrass them.

6. *Don't understand "no."* They often ask for forgiveness and rarely seek permission. The surest way to get them to do something is to tell them they can't do it. "You can't write a great radio commercial for a cheap hotel chain." Huh? Next thing you know, we get Tom Bodett. They are not belligerent about the word, "no." There's nothing malicious about them. It's just not in their nomenclature. They simply don't understand the language of "no."

7. *Laugh, cry, get goosebumps.* Until this last habit, you might be getting the impression that creatives are compulsively driven Fascists devoid of emotion. I've found quite the opposite to be true. Creative people are "feelers." They laugh and cry freely and often. The world gives them goosebumps. They are eternal children. It's how they cope with fear. It's how they deal with success. Every day.

4

EVALUATING TALENT: FIVE TIPS FROM A COACH ON HOW TO SPOT WINNERS

Creative agencies and college athletic programs share one key commonality: their success relies upon recruiting top talent into the fold. Talent is the only true commodity. All other inventory and overhead are a means to the end of attracting and retaining talent (so the agency can attract and retain good clients).

Agencies hire renowned architects and build cool spaces or plush midtown offices. College athletic programs erect shiny new arenas and renovate stadiums with skyboxes. Small and mid-sized regional creative agencies are similar to small and mid-major athletic programs. They have to recruit harder and smarter. They have to evaluate talent more judiciously, and be able to find the diamond in the rough—the talent with upside and desire.

I was a college basketball coach for six years at a mid-major program—Holy Cross College in Worcester, Massachusetts. My primary responsibility was recruiting student-athletes who could compete at high levels in the classroom and on the basketball court. Like mid-sized agencies, there was nowhere to "hide" a recruit that wasn't a good fit (male enrollment: 1,200). If we brought the wrong kid in, not only did it cost us wins, it cost us one of our precious few scholarships. Just like mid-sized agencies, the wrong hire sets the agency back. Evaluating talent becomes the difference between the winners and the losers.

There are two kinds of talent in any field. Let's call them *Original Talent* and *Derivative Talent*. The original talent is one-of-a-kind. Their work and skills are special and distinct—nobody does it quite the way they do it. The derivative talent is skilled and able, but replaceable. Gifted, but not indispensable.

I've found that it's difficult to separate the "game" from the recruit. If a kid plays the game "the right way"—he's probably a solid dude. If he is a shuck and jiver on the court—that's probably the way he is off of it. It's a little trickier with creatives, but it's difficult to separate the person from the portfolio. The trick is to discover if the book matches the recruit.

So how do you do that? What can you do to recruit more smartly and effectively—to evaluate more judiciously?

Here are some things I did as a coach and like to incorporate into my creative recruiting;

1. *The Walk.* Before I'd watch a recruit play in a game, I just wanted to see how he walked. I could tell a lot by that. So I'd get to the gym early to be there for the JV game so I could watch the kid walk into the gym, and then walk into the locker room to dress out. His posture, balance, gait and grace literally signaled how "grounded" he was. I looked for something I call a "humble swagger." All the great ones have this. Some have more of one than the other. But I look for the perfect balance. I was surprised at first that "The Walk" also applied to creative talent—a slouch is a slouch. Greatness begins from the ground up, not the neck down.

2. *Good Hands and a Handshake.* It's amazing how many great athletes can't catch the ball. They can run like banshees and jump out of the gym but throw some of them a pass from eighteen feet with some zip on it and it's concrete city. Coaches that ascribe to "the best available athlete" theory of recruiting often wind up with a team prone to turnovers. So how does this apply to creative agencies? Well, once I pitched a nice piece of NASCAR business to an agency. We had great work, except a creative guy spilled his coffee all over the tissues. I remember another creative guy would develop "the shakes" when he presented work internally and externally. His hands rattled the table. Others always seem to be fumbling stuff. Finally, ever get the dead-fish handshake? It was somewhat in vogue about ten years ago. It creeps me out. Or the Fred Flintstone handshake, where

you need to ice down your hand afterward?

In sport and in business, I want people with sure hands and solid handshakes on my team.

3. *A Peculiar Habit or Trait.* This is pure Palma and impossible to substantiate, just my school of evaluation. I've noticed that the truly great ones—those with Original Talent—ALL have some distinctive peculiar habit or trait. One of the greatest copywriters I've ever recruited chews paper. Another great radio writer had a voyeuristic affinity with a telescope in his office. One of the greatest high school basketball players I've ever seen had this unusual neck tic. In some, it's their dress. In others, their diet. But, behind nearly every great original talent is some distinctive peculiar habit or trait.

4. *Eye Contact.* I'm not a shrink, but I know poor eye contact signals evasiveness or worse, insincerity. As a coach, I would never recruit a kid who didn't look me in the eye. They didn't have to say a lot, but they had to make consistent eye contact. When I recruit a Creative Director for an agency, I make a point to try to meet him. They've got to look me in the eye when they explain why they are motivated by the opportunity. If not, it's lip service.

5. *See Them Sweat.* How are they under adversity? Do they exhibit grace under pressure? Do they handle victory and

defeat with equal dignity? These are key indicators of character. Are they truly competitive? True competitors need to compete, NOT win. Truly competitive people never accept in victory what they would not accept in defeat.

I remember getting numerous VHS tapes of basketball players from all over the country. Invariably they were made by coaches or parents trying to get their kid a scholarship. Besides the obvious "highlights-only" editing, the biggest problem with video evaluation of talent was that you never got to see the kid actually sweat. There is no perspiration on video.

Then when I got into creative recruiting, I received all those three-quarter-inch reels from creative talent. Cassettes. DVD's. When the work was brilliant, I still needed to know that the work was actually the recruit. I needed to "get to the gym early" to see the recruit walk (meet them for coffee, breakfast, etc.). It's a similar dynamic as the creative recruit's portfolio is the "highlights-only" video of the advertising world. It is, too often, accepted as Gospel. We neglect thorough evaluation. They're really good out of the windup but we fail to see them pitch out of the stretch position.

This is where online recruiting really hampers small and mid-sized creative agencies. It leaves them more vulnerable than ever to poor fits. It seems easy: post an ad for a job and count the resumes. The problem is, the top talent—the Original Talent—is not looking on websites for a job.

They're playing. And winning. Online recruiting is shallow and sterile. You get a hundred resumes, 90 of them are blatantly poor fits, and so they get deleted on contact. Ten of them are potential recruits. Now how do you evaluate them? They will be pretty adept on the phone, they're ad people—they know how to talk and sell themselves. I prefer to watch them walk.

The Agency

RECRUITING PRIMER

5

OVERVIEW

So many challenges have confronted the advertising industry in my thirty-five years, perhaps the greatest of which was overcoming the double-whammy recessions of 2002 and 2009—devastating years in our industry akin to the 1929 stock market crash in the financial sector. In case you missed it, the advertising recession of 2002 was first perpetrated by the overinflation of the advertising marketplace due in large part to unrealistic speculation of web-based accounts in late 2000 and early-to-mid 2001.

Then it was exacerbated by the horrific events of September 11th. It became an official recession when we declared war on the Middle East. The last significant advertising recession occurred in 1991, and was also impacted by the declaration of war by the United States. War is good for some industries; advertising is not one of them. This last recession was caused by piggish greed. It was a *credit crisis*.

The Pandemic of 2020 was another monstrous challenge the industry faced. Agency owners balancing PPP loans with furloughs. So much of the pandemic "recession" (which was actually a near-total collapse) was also a credit crisis. We saw companies carrying debt go out of business. Many agencies panicked and cut bait prematurely.

The good news is, if you are reading this, you survived. Congratulations, it wasn't easy. The bad news is that you are left with the fallout of an attrition of talent we are not likely to quickly replace. We are left with an overabundance of junior people. True, advertising has always been a youthful business—but it's never been more youthful than it is today.

What happened at most agencies? Most of the senior management hung on by their fingernails (in many cases taking salary and bonus cuts), very junior people kept their jobs because they were low overhead and a rash of budding mid-to-senior folks were forced out of the industry or into freelance and "perma-lance" domains. To survive we had to cut payroll and, therefore, we created a world of talented consultants. While this fallout still has a major impact on how we actually do business (billing, compensation, etc.), let's focus on how this affects recruiting talent into our industry.

In short, ad agencies have gotten a bad reputation. Once, this was a respectable profession to aspire to. A recent study by JWT revealed that, In terms of respect for the advertising profession, 14 percent of respondents say their fellow Americans respect ad people, besting only "national politicians" (10 percent) and "car salesmen" (5 percent). Re-read this paragraph.

Today, advertising as a career consistently ranks in the lower percentiles in all academic studies of desired professions. Why? We've gotten the reputation that we churn and burn entry-level talent, we sacrifice our developing mid-level talent, and we only care about protecting senior management. This is not exactly the type of industry that will send the best and the brightest of future generations clamoring to work in the mailroom at our agencies, as they did for decades.

We were once an industry that paid well. That perception has changed. We're now known as relative cheapskates compared to other service and consulting industries. And there is little light at the end of the tunnel. Very few agencies train and mentor their young people. It's bad enough that we are no longer attracting the best young junior talent, but we are doing little to develop the ones we are attracting beyond throwing them into the fire.

Somehow, through it all, we've retained a little bit of our "cool factor." Invariably, I ask candidates what they are looking for. Ten to fifteen years ago, the answer was usually "a great opportunity." Today, that answer has morphed into "I'm looking for a cool agency." I'd like to think that it's the same answer by a new generation. But, I think not and that answer is the ultimate trickle-down effect of what our industry is on the verge of becoming: superficial and trivial. Are agencies still cool?

When was the last time an MBA fresh out of Harvard or Wharton or Tuck showed up at your agency and told you this is where he'd like to start his or her career? What's even more alarming is that your business is probably not even structured to hire one if they did.

INDUSTRY, HEAL THYSELF

So, as an industry, we're sick. How do we get better? We have failed to promote ourselves well. Ironic that an industry based on promotion has failed to promote itself properly. This is purely a product of neglect. No bad strategy or flubbed execution. We just neglected our industry trying to survive. The doom loop, as Jim Collins says in *Good to Great*.

Advertising Week in New York is a noble effort toward industry self-promotion. Maybe we can extend the idea as a traveling act and bring it to other cities. The new Diversity Initiatives are a positive sign for our future. But, it almost seems like the advertising industry should hire a PR firm for itself, one that is experienced in crisis management. If we expect to attract the best and the brightest in the prospective employee pool, we need to promote our profession properly, as if it were a client.

Sustainability: There is probably no bigger buzzword out there among our clients than "sustainable." Suddenly, sustainability has become the biggest initiative in the business world today. Clients want us to help them build "sustainable communities" of customers as well as driving business. Products are sustainable. Business models are sustainable. Results are sustainable.

The only thing that hasn't proven to be sustainable is a career in the advertising industry. So how do we create a sustainable career environment? A good place to start is a commitment to training and developing talent. Another is to align our industry with academia. Yet another is to adjust our compensation models to the 21st century (salaries in our industry are essentially what they were in 1991).

A sustainable career environment is one of inclusion and accessibility. We don't value or even need decisions from 80 percent of our workforce. We have created a workforce devoid of the need to make decisions. This is the single greatest factor in job dissatisfaction: "I never get to make decisions" or "my opinions don't matter."

Remember when advertising was a noble career? Well, I don't—but I've seen some old movies that suggest it. Maybe it really isn't, but it's certainly better than how we are perceived today. We are in the business of changing perceptions and if we don't address changing the perception of our own industry we will continue to struggle in attracting top talent into it.

RECRUITING IN THE 21ST CENTURY

One industry that truly relies on great recruiting is college athletics. The universities are brands that have become sustainable communities with a distinct tradition and culture. Athletic programs are investments that manufacture a product (entertainment).

I've always thought that ad agencies—particularly regional, mid-sized agencies—could learn a lot from successful college athletic programs—training, management, planning, and particularly recruiting. The college coach's very survival is inextricably linked to the success of his recruiting efforts. Few ad agencies are committed to bringing in the best possible talent on all levels, through all departments to grow their clients' businesses. Often, agencies hire whom they can to meet their budget and can maintain or keep from losing the existing business.

Approach your recruiting efforts like the head coach of a college sports team. That requires you to evaluate your needs and the existing talent in your marketplace to fill those needs. It requires a recruiting plan, recruiting tools and an unwavering commitment to study the landscape of the industry, and those agencies that are doing the best work and driving the best results. It requires the commitment to do with your agency or department what you say you want to do: hire the best people. That requires you to know the difference.

Agency people are quick to say, "our inventory walks out the door every evening." That kind of thinking commoditized our talent pool. Some people are invariably more talented than others. Some have better attitudes. Some work harder. Some know how to win. Some are better team players than others. "Our inventory" is our intellectual capital. Coaches have a lot of funny sayings when evaluating talent. My favorite is "good enough to get you fired." That line also rings true for evaluating agency talent.

Remember, there are two guarantees in our business:

1. Accounts will come and go.
2. People will come and go.

6

DEFINING ROLES
FOR YOUR TEAM

Most mid-sized regional agencies don't have the luxury of a full-time HR person. Often, the person charged with HR issues is an operational employee, usually doubling as bookkeeper or office manager. This person should not be responsible for agency recruiting. While they can help coordinate recruiting efforts, especially as they relate to policies and guidelines—they should not be responsible for attracting top talent to the agency. In the absence of a full-time agency director, the agency should designate a key management team member as "Recruiting Director." One key person at the agency must own the function and be accountable for agency recruiting since talent is the lifeblood of our business.

In the event that an agency is fortunate enough to require a full-time HR Director, this person assumes the role of Recruiting Director. This role requires:

- Maintaining current and effective agency recruiting tools.
- Keep agency presence current in databases and online trade media.
- Keeping an agency database on top talent in the region, by discipline.
- Maintaining relationships with recruiters and influencers.

THE ROLE OF THE CEO OR PRESIDENT

What's at the top filters down. Very often, the role of recruiting director falls on the shoulders of the president—especially in the world of mid-sized regional agencies. But, the additional role of the president is to establish a culture. There are many articles written about agency *culture.*

Even if you don't want a culture, you have one. Usually, it's the mirror reflection of your clients and their personalities. But, it's the CEO's job to protect it by hiring what "fits." A "fit" can actually be someone who doesn't appear to be a fit. Sometimes the best "fits" are exactly that. That's why you're the CEO, you are supposed to have the wisdom and discernment of a visionary. Visionaries also do their homework.

This role, as it applies to the recruiting process, requires:

- Decisiveness.
- The courage to keep looking.
- Patience in the Flywheel Effect (see *Good to Great*).
- Strict adherence to the agency mission.

- The courage and flexibility to transcend the agency mission through talent.

THE ROLE OF THE MANAGEMENT TEAM

Senior management teams at ad agencies are a lot like assistant coaching staffs at college athletic programs. They form the core of the agency and help shape its direction. Their contribution to agency recruiting, however, is often far too serendipitous. To maximize your management team's network, consider asking them to:

- Be a *"talent scout"* in their discipline.
- Attend trade events and network with rising talent.
- Befriend top specialist recruiters in their discipline.
- Feed resumes to the recruiting director.

THE ROLE OF THE SEARCH FIRM
(THE AGENCY RECRUITER)

Recruiters are a strange breed. But, a good recruiter who understands your culture and your business can save you a lot of time. It might cost a little more than a mid-sized, regional agency cares to spend in fees, but time and talent are the only resources an agency really has. Find one or two in your industry and make them your friends. Good recruiters have been invaluable to virtually every successful agency.

There are two kinds of recruiters:

1. Specialists in filling key senior positions, usually in one specific discipline.
2. Generalists that usually focus on junior-to-mid-level positions across several disciplines.

Good recruiters take the time to understand their client agency's business—their clients' client rosters, their points of differentiation, their case studies and their creative work. They also invest the time in understanding their client agencies' cultures.

The recruiter's duties in the recruiting process:

- To act as an AGENT FOR THE AGENCY, not the candidate.
- Scout and attract the top talent in the industry and understand what will make them move.
- Specialize in one or two disciplines.
- Take a thorough search assignment.
- Present qualified candidates who are sincerely interested in the opportunity.
- Coordinate interviews and telephone screens.
- Debrief candidate and client after interview.
- Negotiate and close the deal.

7

RECRUITING TO WIN: THE SEARCH

Okay, you have a job to fill. For most mid-sized regional agencies, any hire is an important hire. Most agencies follow this path:

1. Look inside their agency first to see if someone can change seats on the agency bus.
2. Call around to agency people they know to see if anyone has recently seen any available talent.
3. Post jobs online hoping to get lucky (this is the "I'm feeling lucky"... I mean, Digital Age).
4. Contact a recruiter when all other paths are exhausted.

Let's explore these steps.

CONDUCTING AN INTERNAL SEARCH

Agencies that train and groom young talent and program them to grow professionally should expect to sometimes fill their needs internally. The best way to go about this is to first ask the employee in a confidential setting if he or she would be interested in making a change and switching responsibilities. The biggest potential problem in many of these cases is that the particular job you are looking to fill comes with a subset of new challenges—and most people are creatures of habit, despite what they say.

In the event of a raise, promotion, or added decision-making opportunities, it is important to gauge if the employee is interested in adding responsibility and not just adding income or a new title. The best internal searches are confidential and narrow; only consider one or two of your current staff—more than that and you are asking for trouble as employees invariably talk to each other—and very often away from the agency. If you decide not to promote one or all—it's likely to leave a trail of disappointment, akin to losing a new business pitch.

Be decisive and stick to deadlines. If you've decided to "open up the search" communicate this to the staffer you have interviewed. The last thing you want is for them to hear this from elsewhere. Don't leave your better people twisting in the wind. It may motivate them to look outside for a similar opportunity as they now are emotionally driven by a promotion or opportunity.

OPEN SEARCHES AND CONFIDENTIAL SEARCHES

The differences appear obvious, but let's look at them.

An open search is when the job is open or soon to be vacated, and it's common knowledge between employee and employer. If you choose, you can ask for referrals, post jobs online, and engage recruiters. This is the case with most agency openings.

But, a confidential search is usually far more critical to the agency. It usually involves:

- A key position to replace an underperforming employee.
- A key employee for a new piece of business that you can't announce.
- A key position to replace an employee that has confidentially resigned.
- Adding a key person to save or shore up an existing account.
- A senior management team member.

In these cases, due to the competitive nature of the agency business, it is always best to conduct a confidential search.

HANDLING EMPLOYEE REFERRALS

Many agencies today have a policy of offering a financial reward to employees if they refer a candidate who is hired by the agency. I'm told by the 4A's that this is popular with agencies and HR types. I guess they believe that they are saving the agency money by not having to pay outside fees. Sometimes, agencies may get lucky this way. In most cases, they are opening a can of worms that come back to haunt them. What if you don't hire a referred candidate by one of your employees? What if you don't even interview them? What kind of message are you sending? What if you hire them and have to pay them more money than the referrer? What if you hire them and it doesn't work out? How do you subvert the feeling that "I got so-and-so his job here and now look...?" You can get lucky, after all, but this policy invariably creates unforeseen problems down the road.

The best way to handle internal referrals is to have your employees forward names on a quarterly basis to your Recruiting Director as potential "fits" for the agency. If you want to offer a financial reward, then reward the employees that refer the best potential "fits," regardless if you hire them or not. Keep these potential "fits" in an active database. They will come in handy.

NETWORKING

It's all about the network. Right? Well, not always. Owners of mid-sized, regional agencies know a lot of connected people. You can often solve a recruiting dilemma by picking up the phone and calling former colleagues and friends. Sometimes, a former colleague or friend will call and make an un-solicited referral. This is recruiting "over the transom."

Sometimes these referrals work out, more often they do not. The worst thing you can do is count on them to consis-tently find your "fits." Obviously, be careful about sending needy messages into the advertising community. Before pick-ing up the phone to make a networking recruiting call make sure the call doesn't expose a vulnerable account or another potential vulnerability at the agency. The odds on networking referrals are long—proceed accordingly.

WORKING WITH A RECRUITER

As a recruiter, I'd like to try to remove partisanship from this section. While recruiting top talent exclusively for adver-tising agencies for thirty-five years, I hope I've gained some insights that can help you recruit more effectively. I'm aware of the perception of recruiters, not only in our industry, but recruiters in general. While we are paid to create win-win situations and solve business problems, we are often viewed as a necessary evil. There are good recruiters, and there are probably bad recruiters. *Find good recruiters.*

How? Take some time and talk to them. It's not that hard to find out who they are. If you don't know who they are, then ask your best people—I guarantee you they know. Talk to them and invite a couple to visit you at the agency. The biggest mis-conception in the universe of agency/recruiter relationships is that recruiters represent candidates and that they are the candidates' agents. This is simply wrong. The recruiter's client is the agency. The agency pays the recruiter. In all cases this is true.

Both agencies and candidates propagate this myth. Candidates sometimes say to me, "I already have a headhunter." It always makes me laugh when I hear that. HR types often ask me, "Are you repping this candidate?" Recruiters don't represent anyone except their client agencies. If this series accomplishes anything, let's at least dispel the myth that recruiters "work" with candidates. They work with agencies to recruit candidates.

This knowledge and mindset empowers you to enlist the top recruiters on your behalf. You may even want to make one your assistant Recruiting Director. It allows you to better understand and control your relationship with recruiters and it allows you to develop your recruiting strategies with your chosen recruiter(s).

There are two ways of working with recruiters:

1. *Contingency.* The most common way of doing business. Fees usually range between 15 percent-30 percent of a candidate's first year salary paid upon start date. You only pay if you hire their candidate. The most common rate in our industry is 20 percent or what you'd pay a good server in a restaurant. Some recruiters charge 25 percent and some others charge 30 percent.

2. *Retainer.* This method is usually for a very key position, a creative director or a management supervisor. It is also common for a confidential search to be handled by a retainer, one where you don't want a lot of recruiters calling a lot of candidates. A retainer is a down payment to the recruiter to buy his time and commitment to the search. It is credited against the overall fee.

Filling a key or senior position usually works better on a retainer. You may get lucky on contingency, but you may wind up paying more in time and money. The best candidates are not looking for a job. They are not surfing the job boards. The top talent is very busy at their jobs, almost impervious to the agency world around them. The best candidates need to be recruited.

The right person and best "fits" for your agency are driving to work this morning with absolutely no inkling of an impending career opportunity. It is the recruiter's job to know this person and know exactly what his "triggers" are. The best recruiters are like Dustin Hoffman in *Rain Man.* They know who the right people are and where they are from (perhaps from a city where one of the recruiter's client agencies is based). They know what the perfect opportunity is for the ideal candidate. Then they sell both sides on the potential fit.

To do this correctly requires time, energy, and a lot of breath. You may find a recruiter qualified and savvy enough to pull this off for you on a contingency basis. But be prepared to seek out an expert and pay them for their time to handle a thorough and professional search. It will be worth it to land the right person.

In filling junior- to mid-level positions, go with the scattershot approach. Engage several recruiters. Play the numbers game. There is strength in numbers, but always stay connected to your lead recruiters and your Recruiting Director. They should have a freezer full of fledgling junior- to mid-level candidates.

And for these positions, posting jobs online may be an effective approach. Again, I wouldn't count on the Internet to solve all your recruiting problems, but maybe a potential "fit" may also be "feeling lucky."

HOW TO ENGAGE A RECRUITER

- Do your homework—discover recruiters who have track records in your universe.
- Talk to them, meet them, educate them about your agency and agency "fits."
- Get fee agreements in writing.
- Set realistic criteria for the search.
- Establish a search strategy and process.
- Stick to it.

HOW NOT TO ENGAGE A RECRUITER

- Have your part-time HR person email them titles and specs.
- Assume he knows the difference between your agency and all others.
- Fight them on fees.
- Ask them to email resumes first.

Remember, the best candidates don't even have a resume. They're working!

8

WHAT TODAY'S TOP TALENT WARS MEAN FOR AD AGENCIES

DON'T BRING A POCKET KNIFE TO A GUNFIGHT

If you haven't noticed on your LinkedIn feed, every day hundreds (if not thousands) of people are hired by advertising agencies. Folks I couldn't get arrested last year are being scooped up by both global and regional shops. If you can fog a mirror, you're hired!

"Hire me!"

There is only one precedent for this kind of hiring activity in my thirty-five years of recruiting experience: the dotcom boom/tech bubble–caused by excessive speculation of internet-related companies in the late 1990s; a period of massive growth in the use and adoption of the newly born world wide web. Back then, even mediocre talent got big raises.

Fast forward to the post-vaccine Roaring '20s.

Well, those then-fledgling tech companies grew up and a few are now the most valuable entities on the planet. So, I have a feeling this bubble will sustain a good bit longer than one in the late- 90's. Get used to that hiring feeling. Why? It's simple math. According to The Wall Street Journal, ad spends are up 19 percent (26 percent in digital). That's a total of $750 billion.

But really, why? We laid off and furloughed so many people in 2020—combine that with the increased workload that comes with nearly 20 percent industry growth and...you get talent wars.

SIGNS OF A TALENT WAR

- Increase in counteroffers accepted
- Significant decrease in jobvite and online applications
- Inflationary salary expectations
- Swollen salaries
- Workplace concessions
- Live/work balance demands
- Remote considerations

So, what does it mean for ad agencies?

- They will have to charge off the inflation to the client or take the hit themselves.

- They will have to get better at the art of recruiting and stop treating hiring top talent as an HR function.
- They will have to go after talent that's not in the "job market"—actually recruit talent instead of waiting for it to fall into their laps.
- They will have to pay real and specific bonuses and incentives.
- They will have to convert the workplace to a live/workplace.
- They will have to go outside of the industry for creative, strategic and account service talent.
- They will have to accept remote and hybrid employees as a partial solution.

In an era of free agency, it's a player's market, not an owner's market. That's the way it should be in an industry with no certification, licenses, or inventory.

9

TWELVE LESSONS IN LEADERSHIP
FROM THE WIZARD

As I mentioned in the opening pages of this, I remember staying up to watch the UCLA vs. Houston game in 1968. It was billed as the "Game of the Century" and was also the first nationally televised college basketball game in prime time, and there were doubts that America would tune in for an amateur product. Although UCLA lost (they wouldn't lose again for 89 games), my life changed that evening. When I learned that these players on television received full college scholarships to *play basketball*—well, it just blew my mind and provided me with my first true goal. I was going to be one of those guys someday.

I loved Lew Alcindor. He hailed from my native New York city-area Catholic school league and he was inordinately tall (likewise, I was a 6-3 by the time I was twelve). I even copied his hook shot. Alcindor was my first basketball idol. He was articulate and opinionated but respectful of the game and his coaches. His 1969 autobiographical *Sports Illustrated* article, "My Story" provided me with my first glimpse into Coach John Wooden. From then on, I read and watched everything I could about the man who was the reason I chose coaching as my first career out of college.

Alcindor spoke with such praise of Wooden—how he helped him become a man. Here was this Brobdingnagian black man from New York City sharing that a hayseed from Indiana taught him what becoming a man was really all about.

Much has been written of Wooden's Pyramid of Success. It would serve your agency well if you hung it up somewhere for your colleagues and employees to see. I am most inspired by Wooden's 12 Lessons in Leadership:

1. Good values attract good people.
2. Love is the most powerful four-letter word.
3. Call yourself a teacher.
4. Emotion is your enemy.
5. It takes 10 hands to make a basket.
6. Little things make big things happen.
7. Make each day your masterpiece.
8. The carrot is mightier than the stick.
9. Make greatness attainable by all.
10. Seek significant change.

11. Don't look at the scoreboard.
12. Adversity is your asset.

Business Development

GETTING NEW CLIENTS
FOR YOUR AGENCY

10

POSITIONING YOUR CREATIVE AGENCY FOR GROWTH AND HOW TO GET TO YOUR VALUE PROPOSITION

I hear and see so much about agency positioning these days. It seems as if agencies are constantly re-inventing themselves to adapt to market conditions. When discussing a positioning for a creative agency, I've found it helpful to consider these three questions first:

- Who are you?
- Why are you different?
- What does that mean to your clients' or prospects' business?

These questions should lead the discussion and bring some clarity and simplicity to the process. Positioning a creative agency for growth is an arduous and daunting task. Without the proper structure and road maps it can also lead to frustration, bitterness and, worst of all, paralysis.

Can you articulate who you are in one or two sentences? Can you explain why you are different—truly different—in ONE sentence? NOT how you *think* you are different—but the reality of your point of differentiation. Do you have a point of differentiation? Finally, do you understand your value—what it means to your clients' businesses? Do you have a value proposition? Can you state it simply? Can you articulate it in an interesting way? In a creative way? Your value proposition will be at the core and essence of your positioning.

Let's look at what a value proposition is NOT:

- A process. It's not a TM of some special proprietary mystery procedure.
- A self-promotional rally cry, also TM'd.
- A place or region ("Texas-sized solutions").
- People. Talent is not a positioning. Everyone says they have the best people.
- Products. Cookie-cutter solutions. Offerings. Widgets. Technology. Disciplines.
- A Mission.
- Creative or "Creative-driven." This is assumed. It's like ketchup brands talking about being "tomato-driven."

All of these elements are part of a creative agency's value proposition, but none of them can stand-alone or hold up as *the positioning*. Worse, over-reliance on any one of these elements becomes oversimplification. A position should be as simple as possible, but not one bit simpler (paraphrasing Albert Einstein).

When embarking on any positioning exercise, go back to basics. I like referencing Jim Collins' *Good to Great*. This bestseller is on the bookshelf of every CEO in America. Most have implemented its recommendations at their companies. It has been the "positioning bible" of the past decade.

I remember in 2004 at BBDO, we were pitching Delta Air Lines. When we advanced to the final three, their CEO Jerry Grinstein sent the agency two copies of *Good to Great*. Until then, I kind of scoffed at business books that claimed to solve company-wide issues and problems in one easy read. Then I learned that MOST CEOs of major companies were forming *hedgehog councils* and treating Collins' tome as gospel. Marketing directors began talking about *Bhags*.

The crux of *Good to Great* is the Hedgehog Concept.[1] Picture a Venn diagram with three circles, each containing a question. At the top, *what are you deeply passionate about?* In the lower right, *what drives your economic engine?* In the lower left, *what can you be the best in the world at?*

While Collins uses the word "world" in the lower left circle, we can effectively substitute the word "class" or even "region." What is your agency best-in-class at? Or what can your creative agency be "best-in-class" at? What can you own with-

---

1   Collins, Jim. "The Hedgehog Concept." Jim Collins - Concepts - The Hedgehog Concept. Accessed August 12, 2024. https://www.jimcollins.com/concepts/the-hedgehog-concept.html.

in your class? What positioning is unique and "own-able?" *If it is not own-able, it's not a powerful positioning.* That does not include "shareable" or "borrowable."

What are you uniquely passionate about? What drives your economic engine (where do your clients place the most financial value)? What can you be the best at within your class? Dialogue centered on these questions leads to lively discussions and healthy debates. Monday morning meetings are ideal for engaging in such banter. At some point, you need to put a strategic stake in the ground. Don't allow these positioning discussions to dissipate into paralysis of analysis. That happens easily when the first client emergency arises on your desk.

There are, essentially, two kinds of agency archetypes:

• Those that solve problems (stop the bleeding).
• Those that create opportunity (add revenue).

The first type requires COLLABORATION. These agencies stress collaborative processes. They reflect their clients' cultures. They are problem-solvers; therefore they need to understand the problems. They speak the client's language. They are not usually entrepreneurial or independent. They stay in the present and address the now. They ask questions like, "What keeps you awake at night?" and "What are your marketing objectives?".

The second requires LEADERSHIP. These agencies stress thought leadership and cultural "curation." They are opportunists, therefore they need to understand potential. They take risks (educated and strategic risks, but risks nonetheless). They make language new for their clients. They have their own culture. They are independent and maverick. Because they are ahead of the curve, they create revenue opportunities for their clients. They make them money. They ask questions like, "What is your vision for your brand?" and "What's the one thing you would do for your brand if you thought it was possible?"

Most agencies try to be both. And as a result, they are neither. Of course, both types of agencies are collaborative *and* leaders in various junctures of the marketing process. But I'm talking about how they tell their story and what they do best—that's their value proposition. Identify what your creative agency does best. Where do you shine? Where do you play best? In short, don't pick a fight you can't win.

If you remain steadfast and disciplined in your positioning discussions, you will arrive at an insight that is compelling. You will discover your true identity. It will be an epiphany. It will give you goosebumps. It will be that *a ha* moment. The germ of your insight will lead naturally to your positioning.

But, start by trying to answer the three questions:

- Who are you?
- Why are you different?
- What does that mean to your clients' and prospects' business?

11

AGENCY POSITIONING
IN A SEA OF SAMENESS

The beautiful thing about language is that it catches on. When folks find a befitting phrase that captures their circumstance, it can take on a life of its own. And at the tipping point, it becomes a phenomenon. This was the case with the phrase "voracious reader." Somehow, anyone with three paperbacks on their nightstand in the 1990's was suddenly a "voracious" consumer of the written word. The phrase took on a slight tone of literary condescension (most condescension is slight and subtle). For example, if you had a *Sports Illustrated* magazine on your nightstand, you really didn't qualify as a voracious reader. To qualify as truly voracious, one was required to juggle several titles at a time from the New York Times bestseller list.

Rather than attack all the similar things ad agencies say

about themselves ("best-in-class," "fully integrated," etc.), let's just take a look at a currently persistent one: *fiercely independent*. I know, it sounds so cool and maverick. It screams, "we're such tough hombres." There are two problems with "fiercely independent." The first is, it's redundant to the point of weakness.

Adjectives can be dangerous like that. Secondly, it's become such a common theme among independent agencies that it's lost all effectiveness as a point of differentiation. But, certain phrases are simply irresistible.

W. Somerset Maugham said, "Money is the string with which a sardonic destiny directs the motion of its puppets." Independent agencies attempt to connect their business brevity to a tangible financial benefit for the prospective client. In other words, you don't have to pay a percentage to a holding company. I suppose that kind of claim may be an endearing approach with Procurement. But not a single marketer in history has ever been fired because they retained a holding company agency. Conversely, LinkedIn is littered with former client-side VPs who took a chance on the latest independent creative Hothouse. Clients buy great creative that works. At the end of the day, it doesn't matter to them where their money goes. Price doesn't matter. It never did and it never will.

Go ahead and google "fiercely independent ad agency." The search reveals no fewer than 27 agencies—some of which are among the best-known in the industry. One is actually an

IPG agency that claims to be "fiercely independent" but can also "instantly" enlist "an army of 23,000" people through an "odd twist." They conclude their positioning with "who we are depends on what you need." Now that's what I call putting a stake in the ground. As the inimitable Tim Bayless often cackled, "We have our principles—and if you don't like those, we have plenty of others in the back."

The moral of the story is stop talking about independence and be independent. Lead your clients fearlessly. Stop selling on price and get to the real tangible benefit of your agency to your clients' businesses: you make them money, not save them money.

12

THE SAUSAGE FACTORY: TMI IN THE AGE OF INFORMATION

You have a medical condition, a hernia. You know something is definitely wrong with your body—it's not performing properly. So you go to the doctor.

What does he do? Does the doctor show you X-rays of previous hernia patients? Does he waste your time by walking you through his track record of success in performing hernia operations? Does he show you what those other patients are doing now? How they are performing as a result of his operative techniques? And does the doctor try to convince you to get an operation because of his proprietary hernia procedures? We would think that the doctor wasn't very good if he had to make a case study to perform a hernia operation. We would seek a second opinion.

Or, let's say you want sausage for dinner so you go to a pork store (when I was a kid, there was a "pork store" or Italian butcher in every neighborhood). Does the butcher take you to the back of the store and say, "Here's where we take the gizzards and chop them up. And these are the casings that we stuff the fat and chopped organs into. Our casings are made of the finest pig intestines." If this happened, you might never eat sausage again.

Yet, ad agencies feel compelled to show X-rays to prospective clients and give them a tour of the sausage factory. Why? It's easier than diagnosing a particular patient's hernia or the prospect's particular problem. We show them what we have done for others and not what we can do for them. We stamp trademarks on "secret sauce" processes as if they are anything more complicated than making sausage.

Don't get me wrong. It's a rare and true art to make a great sausage. It requires time-tested recipes involving caraway seeds and special spices. But, the sausage maker knows that only two things really matter to his customers: taste and price. The Italian butcher doesn't say, "Well, if that's what you want to pay for the sausage, then I will make them smaller." He sets his price and makes his sausage. Then he sells them because his customers like the way they taste.

It's the same with great creative communications. Remember the TV show on AMC called *The Pitch*? I've never watched *Mad Men* so I don't really understand this emerging public fascination with the advertising business. It's really quite unsensational, the day-to-day of it; much like the butcher's day.

This comes from Carey Moore, one of the great Southern copywriters of our era, "If you rolled the cameras and re-created a typical week in a creative department, it would be the most boring television ever made. What we actually do isn't very glamorous to a cold set of eyes. They had to make it contrived to make it even remotely watchable."

I visit agencies ALL THE TIME. Between business development and headhunting, I've been inside well over a thousand agencies in the past thirty-five years. Ad agencies are quiet, like a library (more so now than ever). They are sterile, like a hospital. They are politically correct, like a government agency. They are fashion-backward (jeans & Clarks), like a college campus. Yes, the babes are hot, but besides that, there is nothing remotely entertaining about the advertising business—EXCEPT THE PRODUCT (at the better creative agencies, that is). Shows like *Mad Men* and *The Pitch* create a false illusion about our industry—show business replaces sound business sense. Creativity becomes a cliché, marginalized in a sea of strategy and soap opera voyeuristic sexcapades.

Does our industry really need this type of promotion? No wonder it's so hard to find a good young writer today. Everyone wants to be this Don Draper guy. But, the smart kids are going to work for the top consulting firms, like Boston Consulting Group. And, as a result, BCG and the like are writing the real business and marketing strategies for clients today.

They view us as narcissistic dilettantes. They warn our clients away from us. This explains to me why talent agencies like Creative Artists Agency have infringed upon advertising creative territory. They've become more creative than us and produce better work. We go to *Mad Men* cocktail parties and watch ourselves on *The Pitch*.

Clients aren't buying into it. They remark to me about how offended they are by agency case studies. "It's like the brand never could have succeeded without them," one recently told me. Their "douche radar" beeps loudly when agencies tout their trademarked proprietary processes and the fancy phrases they coin to promote themselves, er, explain their point of differentiation. They don't want to see X-rays—they want their hernia fixed.

Don't show them gizzards. Show them the sausage.

13

THE CASE STUDY
DECONSTRUCTED

AD AGENCIES ARE REALLY SMART...
JUST ASK THEM

We have descended deeply into the age of the irrefutable, fool-proof, "look-at-us" Ad Agency Case Study. Today, we have video case studies, digital case studies, printed case studies and a neat, new tool-du-jour, the Infographic.

Funny, I worked in the ad agency business throughout the entire 1990s and never once heard the term "Case Study" in our industry. It's actually a phrase that I first became familiar with through my love for mid-century furniture—it's called "case study furniture" and Charles Eames was the first designer I noticed to use these two words together. Today, one cannot visit an agency website without being bombarded by "case studies" at every click. How did we get here, people? One day we wake up, and all of a sudden, we're so smart (just ask us).

This trend coincides with the "de-construction" of seemingly everything from my nachos and lasagna to clothing. At the risk of sounding like Andy Rooney, excuse me, but I actually want my lasagna *constructed*. And as an agency biz dev person, I want my successes understated. I don't want to tell prospects that I am "integrated," I want to show them. In fact, I don't want to tell them very much at all. I want to SHOW them. And then I want them to TELL ME what they need.

So in the spirit of deconstructionism, let's take a look at the modern ad agency case study. There seems to be a particular template that most agencies follow. The boilerplate formula usually goes something like this:

Challenge > Insight > Tactics > Result

Sounds logical, huh? Let's just spell out for everyone how smart we are. Let's show them our chops. Here's how it usually looks and sounds:

CHALLENGE

When Acme Corporation came to us...
(actually, you harassed them for three years and finally, to get you off his back, a lowly Product Manager handed you the

biggest turd on his desk)

they were really up shit's creek

(even if the client "approves" your case study, does anyone really want the world to know they have problems? Does any client want to show their vulnerability to the competition? Or where they may become vulnerable again in the future? That lowly product manager might have approved your case study, but by the time it's revealed to the CMO and ultimately, the CEO, you just got your product manager fired or put on double-secret probation).

Acme was faced with an unprecedented problem in their long and distinguished history.

(gasp!)

Wile E. Coyote had smartened up and wasn't falling for the Roadrunner's old tricks anymore. Mr. Coyote figured out that there was real dynamite in those packages marked "Acme Corporation."

(yes, the target is smarter than ever, duh)

So, their challenge to us was monumental: Engage Mr. Coyote in a conversation and make him believe, despite the treacherous implications of dynamite, that we feel his pain.

sounds like fast food advertising, or alcohol, or just fill in the blank with a category from your client roster

The challenge was to make Mr. Coyote proud to be part of a club that blows itself up every chance it gets.

Let's just reveal our client's strategy to their competition, while we're at it

INSIGHT

So, we conducted bookoo research on coyotes throughout North America

(for bookoo dollars)

guided by our proprietary planning model that we call Exact-amundo/trademark.

(spare us all the TM, please)

Our research

(which pretty much confirmed Acme's existing research into coyotes)

led us to the startling realization that coyotes really don't like to blow themselves up. They may like the smell of explosives, and the taste of explosives, but at their core—they are tired of the lingering effect of explosives. So out of this realization we stumbled upon the completely unexpected insight that "coyotes are not as dumb as we think they are." And we profiled our target coyote and named him "the wily coyote."

(gasp, what a clever name!)

TACTICS

Since Acme is outspent four to one by their competition

(let's just tell the whole world that they are cheapskates, as well as unsophisticated marketers that don't know how to apply their own research)

we had to make every dollar work like four. To do this, we called in all of our vendor and media chits and basically stiffed a bunch of freelancers with slow-pays. No big deal, they're more desperate than we are. But, to trick the target coyotes into thinking that we aren't actually advertising to them, we built a Facebook page devoted to these smarmy, tech-savvy Wily Coyotes. We figured if we could talk to our core, and invite others to listen in, we could grow a cult. On the Facebook page, we put up a viral video of old Roadrunner cartoons. We knew that if we could get the coyotes to laugh at themselves, then they wouldn't mind blowing themselves up again. It would be funny. And nostalgic. And reto-kitschy. Social media drove the campaign, but we also built a video game called "Coyote Ugly" which we drove awareness through Outdoor Boards on deserted highways throughout the Midwest and the Mojave desert. These boards were ridiculously cheap media buys. The boards appear below—our favorite one is the headline, "You'll Never Catch Roadrunner, Dumb Coyote."

RESULTS

At last count, while we wait for the conclusive results, we've pretty much re-defined the American food chain. While we knew that could happen, we didn't expect to crack the genetic code, as well—which was also an unintended effect of the campaign. Acme same store explosive sales are up 39 percent, they have two million Facebook "likes" and 3 million YouTube hits. Acme is no longer a client, so we're free to do the same for your brand. Call us, we're hungry for your business.

14

A NEW APPROACH TO
AD AGENCY NEW BUSINESS

SEVEN MYTHS TO AVOID

1. *New Business is a Numbers Game.* Bah, humbug. Less is more. Pick 15 Primary Prospects and fifteen backups. Out of the 15 primaries, pick five as your highest priorities. Treat them as if they are already clients. Bring them ideas. Recruit them. Stop spamming the world with your newsletter. Nobody cares about your blog. Let's get over that nonsense and get back to intelligent, personalized agency outreach.

2. *Clients Want Category Specialists.* Nah. Clients want great creativity built upon unexpected insights and great service. They assume you will understand their business and

their category. This specialization theory that runs rampant today is not a point of differentiation... it's a point of sameness. "We're experts in your category"—could you be more pompous, maybe? Category specialization may get you into a pitch, but it will NEVER win you an account.

3. *Size Matters.* Oh, yeah? Tell that to Barton F. Graf 9000 or Baldwin& or Made in Boulder. Creativity matters. Clients want six key people on their account, not 200.

4. *Social Media Creates Inbound Marketing.* Sure, it does. Tweeting out your agency propaganda brings in tire-kickers by the barrel. 999 out of 1,000 "inbound" leads are crap, admit it.

5. *Clients Seek Collaboration.* That's what they say. But, they really want leadership that listens. Anyone can collaborate; but, few can lead. And even fewer can lead through breakthrough creative. Collaboration is table stakes. Stop selling collaboration and start leading.

6. *Agencies Are Marketing Partners.* Stop drinking your own Kool-Aid. Agencies are vendors. You earn marketing partnerships after you help that client achieve business results. Stop selling your agency as a "partner." Think about how you would feel if a candidate on a job interview claimed they would be a partner at your agency. Partnership is earned, not claimed.

7. *Price Matters.* No, it doesn't. It never did, and it never will. If they have to ask what it costs, they can't afford it. If they want a volume discount, send them to Costco. Do your homework upfront and stop recruiting cheapskate prospects. Professional Marketing Services are costly. Great creative is expensive. Sell quality.

15

TURNING THE RFP PROCESS AROUND: HOW CREATIVE AGENCIES CAN CONTROL THEIR OWN FATE

You are a maverick. You have your own creative business or career. That's a fairly intangible and subjective commodity. You survive and advance on guile. You succeed through desire—the greatest of all inspiration. You grow serendipitously, through good work and karma.

At the end of every year, you wonder not only "how did it go by so fast?", but also "how can I keep this up?" It's not a game for kids, selling creative ideas that sell. You understand the difference between creating content and communicating. You know how to communicate well and effectively for your clients. Yet you are too busy or modest to do this for your own business or career—often preferring to "let the work speak for itself." It sometimes does, but it often remains silent.

You are not a conformist. Yet, you conform to the rules of engagement for agency growth. You comply with the RFP process. This is unlike you. It quietly eats away at you—particularly in a pitch against agencies that you know you are a better fit than. You put yourself in this position. You played the game. You played by the rules. You allowed everyone to level the playing field. You allowed yourself to look and sound the same as everyone else.

You are supposed to be a creative agency and yet you let creative "speak for itself" in the engagement process. You did nothing creative about the creative. Did you think all clients could tell the difference?

You have a chance to do something about it. You can begin by first vowing to take fate into your own hands. Then you can pick five to fifteen companies/brands/clients you KNOW you can help and should be working with (no more than three in any one category). Then you can tell them why.

As it stands now—you are just playing the new business game, responding to RFPs, kissing consultants' asses, and bringing in some smile-and-dial monkey or some of the new Twitterati to blog and tweet your way to fame and fortune. You realize tweeting for new business is just a technologically advanced form of "cold calling." Whatever you want to call it—you're at the mercy of unknown forces. That is NOT controlling your own fate.

You can tell them why they should be working with you in a creative way. You can tell them why in their own language, in their own format. You can send them an RFP. Why not? They have no problem sending you an RFP. Why can't you return the favor? If nothing else, it will get their attention and you will stand out from the pack. If the RFP is crafted and worded intelligently with relevant and insightful questions, you will score more points than directing them to your website or blog. Your insights should be unexpected and dramatic based on the homework and research you've done on that particular brand and its category.

You are a maverick.

Act like one.

16

NEW BUSINESS
IN THE NEW WORLD: EIGHT TIPS

This is not meant to be some pep talk. In the new world, the temptation is to try to provide inspiration. I believe nobody can claim to have any or all of the answers for anything right now. That's quite a mouthful for someone that does not believe in absolutes.

What has happened around the world in the past month or so is only unbelievable if you believed in the infallibility of mankind. So let's begin with the acknowledgment that nobody is an "expert" at anything. Let's start anew in humility.

Smugness will surely backfire. The last four disasters to inflict pain upon the advertising industry brought with them a degree of smug: "I choose not to participate in the recession" crap. This is different. This is life or death.

This is the time for leaders to lead. If your agency hangs its hat on collaboration—you're already irrelevant. If you have not led your clients by now, it's probably too late. But if you have, it's time to take your fate completely into your own hands. It's time to stop waiting on referrals. It's time to stop chasing RFPs. It's time to get proactive. Today.

These times require a new approach; not just to new business, but to your business. Here are some thoughts that might work for you, especially if you are a small-to-midsize, regional, creative agency—the salt of the agency earth. This new approach is based upon NOT being an "advertising agency" but instead, a business consultancy that can execute with creativity.

- *Vocation-based outreach.* Now is not the time to sell your agency's benefits to prospects or or clients. No, it's the time to rescue businesses through your *knowledge and* expertise. Think of yourself as a "business doctor"—be a consultant and not an ad person. I remember in 2001 when the Twin Towers went down; the airline industry ground to a halt. So, the great Paul Cappelli took an idea to JetBlue. He gave it to them for free. It helped that a fledgling airline in its infancy literally survive. And when the economy recovered, guess what? JetBlue hired Cappelli's tiny Ad Store as AOR. The lesson? Make your agency crisis-relevant. All brands and industries are facing unprecedented challenges in the near term. It's time to truly be a giant slayer now.

Do it through ideas. When you call a prospect and they say, "But, we already have an agency" be prepared to reply, "That's OK, you can still have our idea. We'd like to execute it, but whatever is best for you." Be the hired gun they don't have. The big agencies cannot move and think like this. You can.

- *Location-based meetings.* Charity begins at home. Pick twenty to thirty regional businesses within 180 miles that you *know* you can help with an idea. Now is not the time to fight for agency compensation or put a stake in the ground around your principles. It is time to do good for your business community by way of your talents and skills. It's time for you to do the right thing.

- *Personal prospecting.* Think through how your current clients and prospects can be relevant now and in the very near future. What can they do to lead? Write each prospect a personal email; no more Campaign Monitor or MailChimp-type generic mass emails bragging about how great your agency is. Instead, write them a personal email and TELL THEM YOU HAVE AN IDEA FOR THEIR BUSINESS. Ask if you can set up a 15-minute call (no in-person meetings) to present your idea. Ask them if they would prefer Skype, but all you really want to do is talk to them.

- *Back off the Data for now.* No data nor any precedent exists for global pandemics; unless you were around in 1918. If you choose to sell your data chops now, it has to be real-time beta testing. But, selling data might weaken the strength of your proposed idea. Do not confuse being humble with squishiness. You may have to use your instincts now. Some of you relish that challenge.

- *Present versatile ideas.* Just because your prospecting is personal, your idea can be broad, industry-specific and category-wide. Study and learn from every brand's corporate tweets. That's where their communication priorities lie. I suspect those tweets may be fairly consistent across the category.

- *Present uncomplicated ideas.* Make sure your ideas are easily executable and operationally simple. The client or prospect should be able to respond, "we can do that right now." A lot of production shoots are being delayed, so if you've invested in an onsite content studio, you have an advantage.

- *Back off the CMO.* Maybe we should work from the bottom up. Those young and flexible Brand Managers and Associate Marketers might be able to push your idea upwards and to the top. They love being heroes. And they are trying to save their jobs. Give them the ammo.

- *Be empathetic.* This is more important than ever.
  So, what happens when you get this "meeting" confirmed?

- Stick to the fifteen-minute timeframe.

- Abandon credentials, case studies and creative samples. Nobody wants to be pitched with your agency deck right now.

- Stick with one simple but big business idea for them.

THE NEW MEETING

- This is who you are and what your brand means. This is why you exist. Tell them why their brand is important.

- This is why we want to help you.

- These are your particular challenges right now.

- This is our idea for you.

- Be prepared to discuss an execution plan if they ask you "how do we do this?" Be prepared to outline the next steps.

- Remind them that they have a duty and responsibility to communicate with their customers and the world.

IF THE MEETING IS ON SKYPE

- Dress professionally. Look like a consultant.

- Rehearse your call.

- Have IT in the room in case there's a glitch. There's no time to joke around about your technological shortcomings.

- Be precise and surgical; you are a business doctor.

- No time to joke around. Build the relationship through your ideas.

Finally, help your fellow agencies if you can. Be part of something bigger than your own little office. Be part of a noble industry. We can change the perception of our industry through this crisis. Look at this as an opportunity. Tap into your Association—the 4A's. They exist to help you. Be a part of a "task force" to help guide your fellow agencies through the rest of 2020. We are all in this together.

17

TWENTY THINGS TO DO
FOR A NEW BUSINESS

1. Skip breakfast, it's the least important meal. If you want to win new business, you've got to be hungry.

2. Don't go to lunch until you've connected with a new business target.

3. Send one handwritten letter every day to a prospect—make it a love letter about their brand.

4. Send one email every day warning another prospect about their mortal enemy.

5. Get closer to your agency's "why."

6. Get away from your agency's "how" and "what."

7. Take out a job order for your agency's Infographic—have your best designer do it.

8. Take out a job order for your agency's one-minute video based on your agency's "why"—produce that video in thirty days—have your best writer write it.

9. Take every image and every word off your website's landing page except the video and the infographic.

10. Join the 4A's. If you are already a member, commit to education from the top down at your agency.

11. Outsource your transom, not your outreach.

12. Kill the category lists.

13. Pick thirty prospects—join every prospect's LinkedIn Groups.

14. Publish on LinkedIn once every week.

15. Slay an evil giant with communications—get famous that way.

16. Write your book—the book the marketing world can't live without (if you can't do this, get out of the business now). Buy the title URL on GoDaddy.

17. Set up a blog at that URL—post every Tuesday and Friday.

18. Repost that post on LinkedIn as a published article.

19. Pump the post into your LinkedIn groups.

20. Send an RFP to 2 prospect companies—make them apply for a spot on your client roster.

18

BUILDING A BALANCED, ORGANIC PROSPECT LIST

Let's take a timeout from the outreach and look at how to build your list. In building a manageable list—say forty prospects—you will chart a road map that will lead you to your top five Prospects. We know those top five should get 80% of your attention, but that leaves 50% of your time unaccounted for (Yogi Berra math). More importantly, it broadens your bandwidth and increases your odds. Everyone knows to establish criteria and emphasize category experience. Yes, you can approach several prospects in the same category with the same unexpected insight or business idea.

One of the most interesting things I learned working on the agency side was the role that planners played in determining the sweet spot target audience for their clients. I loved the way they profiled demos and anointed the target with pithy titles—"The Discount Diva" for Song Airlines was my favorite. The planners established target criteria, set up a prism and fed different profiles through the prism. I'm a bit surprised that agencies don't do more of that for themselves—you know, run basic research on their targets and feed them through an account planning prism (maybe some do—I've just never heard anyone talk about it yet). Well, that's the way I started to approach prospecting—set criteria, build a prism and run prospect profiles through it.

Lee Lynch built a pretty good creative agency at Carmichael Lynch. Someone once showed me his new business triangle on a napkin. I lost the napkin but built my pyramid around an adaptation of Lynch's triangle.

It looks like this and is fairly self-explanatory.

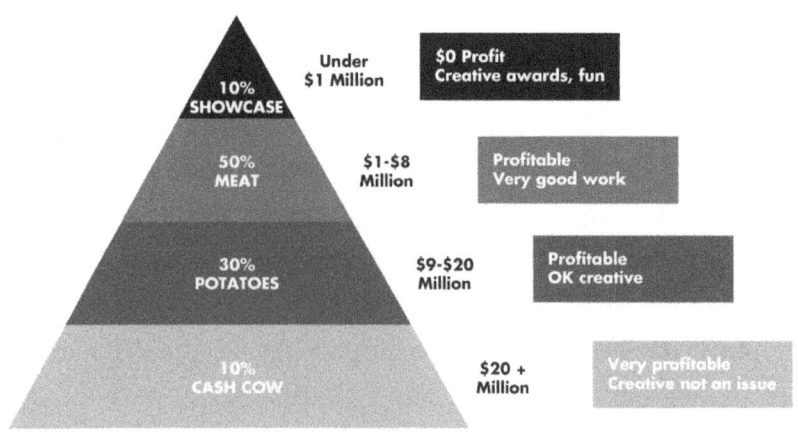

Establishing & Refining Criteria for Prospecting

PALMA PROSPECT PYRAMID

It's important for agencies to have a balanced client roster. It's healthier, better for morale, and better for their clients. It's more conducive to fresh ideas and uncluttered thinking. It rejects cookie-cutter solutions. I know that opinion flies in the face of the conventional wisdom of promoting your agency as narrow specialists—but didn't Bogusky give a rousing keynote on the merits of defying convention—on breaking the rules?

If you were a basketball coach, you would have a very difficult time winning with five point guards. Or five centers. Or five rebounders. You need all those things to win, but the great teams are balanced. Therefore, I think it's important to have a balanced prospect list. One key point on the pyramid is to realize that your top five prospects will come out of the "meat" grouping. This group represents half of your total prospect list.

Again, everyone knows the basic criteria: category, geography, demographics, revenue, etc. Lately, I've had the most success with another criterion. I don't have a pithy name for it, but a great way to build a relationship with a marketer is to "live" their brand. Those prospects' brands are in your closet, your garage, your refrigerator and your liquor cabinet. They're on your American Express statement and your bank drafts. Ask your new business council to run an audit on the brands they live with and make a list. You can speak with conviction to these prospects. You can lead an exciting conversation. Exciting conversations are memorable. This is organic prospecting—not shaking down your existing clients for more money.

I know the new wisdom is to dumb everyone down into being category "experts" (geez, how pompous). I've heard all the fear mongering, "clients are afraid, they want 'safe'... they want round pegs for round holes". Reminds me of fashionistas who say, "never wear plaid and stripes together" or foodies that won't mix red wines with seafood. Is there anything less interesting than a *matchy-matchy* person? I've also seen how some search consultants construct their RFPs. Part of their service is to eliminate the guesswork. I believe that when smart marketers seek creative solutions, a little art appreciation is required—it's not a pure science or math.

Regardless, most small-to-midsize creative agencies will never see the shadow of a search consultant, no less an RFP from one—so don't prospect accordingly. The real truth is that the last thing your best people want to work on is another account in your cash cow category. And on the prospect side, you will be eliminated from consideration due to a perceived conflict within your "expert category" at least as many times as a prospect will value category experience. The best prospects want fresh ideas anyway. They want to stand out and defy category conventions. They want to be a category of "one."

19

NEW BUSINESS,
COLD CALLING, AND GOLF

I've been reading about a business development conference in New York. Four hundred members of the agency new business community convened to learn new trends and tricks for their professional education. Unfortunately I wasn't able to attend due to a new business pitch.

It wasn't unexpected to hear about the overwhelming emphasis placed on digital/social media outreach in new business prospecting.

It alarms me somewhat that social media is being touted as the driver of a new "paradigm" of business development prospecting. I've been around for more than a few "new paradigms" in new business—the very phrase is such a cliché that it undercuts the credibility of any new idea or tactic. I am WAY open to any new way of succeeding in business development. But, I am leery of any proposed shortcuts or ABSOLUTES in the discipline. I use social for my clients, and digital...but it augments the program, it doesn't drive it. I look at digital/social as great ways to pave the road for the driver—the real driver though is your personal ability to establish a business relationship with the prospect.

I read a somewhat disturbing quote from the conference, *"Cold calling for new business is terrible. It's like golf, you stink for 17 holes then hit one good shot and it sucks you back in."* Whoa. To begin with, I don't stink at golf. I'm a single-digit handicap. I've played the best courses in the world. I've made holes-in-one. I've won tournaments.

At one time in my life, I DID stink at golf. Everyone does when they begin. I didn't like that. So I decided to do something about it. Golf was important enough to me to want to improve to a level of competitiveness and respectability within my peer group. MY PEER GROUP IS AGENCY PRINCIPALS AND MARKETING DIRECTORS.

I took lessons to learn the proper techniques and I practiced instilling these techniques until I had the confidence to trust my swing. I began thinking of myself as a good golfer. Therefore, I became one. No shortcuts, no magic potions or miracle equipment. Certainly, like "cold calling," it has its humbling days. But, that's what makes incremental success so rewarding.

Why would you think you would NOT stink at golf if you only play a few times a year and consider yourself a terrible golfer? Would you expect to be a good pianist if you played the piano five times a year? Or more tellingly, if you practiced the piano five times a week, but you hit the same wrong keys every day would you expect to improve? If you put enough monkeys in front of enough typewriters would one of them write a Shakespearean sonnet? No. Seems frustrating for the agency management type who goes out to his client's fund-raiser golf outing a few times a year and hacks it up to the point of embarrassment.

Here's the one beautiful thought you can take solace in if you do hit that one great shot on 18 and it "sucks you back in": *if you hit that one shot properly, you can do it again, and again.* Maybe not every time, but a lot of the time. You just need to find out what you did right and repeat the swing. This takes lessons and practice. Repetition instills confidence.

Now, about cold calls. First of all, a savvy agency business development professional doesn't make "cold" calls. They make two types of calls:

• A relationship-building business call.

• A professional marketing call with a tangible benefit for the prospect.

This is a big-ticket sale with an extended cycle and time-line. If you are calling prospects with the goal of "closing" them on a pitch meeting in one call, you are in the wrong industry. That happens as often as an eagle in golf. "Cold" calls

are for telemarketers driving small-ticket or low-interest purchases. They are one-call closers. It takes an array of outreach
to our prospects to get a meaningful meeting. Yes, digital and
social are part of this mix. It's not either/or—it's *and.*

The New York conference's premise of this supposed
"new paradigm" of business development outreach through
social media is that "80 percent of all transactions begin with
an online search." Really? All transactions? So we are lump-
ing an agency's creative product with buying a pair of shoes
on Zappos? Or are we equating our agency's strategic offering
to illegal Viagra from Canada? Same metrics, I guess. I never even considered agency compensation as a "transaction"
anyway. It's a big-ticket sale.

Hey, do the social media thing.

Digital/social tools allow us to learn about our prospects
and help them learn about us. We can learn a great deal
about the prospects as people through their social profiles.
But, to think someone will cut us monthly checks for huge
sums of money because they like our blog is pretty vain. With
LinkedIn and Facebook, there is really no reason for us to
make a truly "cold" call. We don't have to ask inane questions
like "What's your background?" anymore. And by just being
a good guy with a respectful POV on someone's business or
attending trade shows, we can even become Facebook friends
or LinkedIn connections with our prospects. Then we have a
basis for a real connection. When I make a marketing call, my
number one goal is to be MEMORABLE. I want that prospect

to think, "I've never gotten a call like this."

A memorable professional business marketing call can only be made after doing the necessary homework on the prospect's business, and it needs to be delivered with an unexpected insight into the prospect's category or customer. This is like practicing putting in golf. You need to put the ball in the hole or all the technique is for naught. Practice is a means to an end—the end is the confidence and expertise you communicate to a prospect. This is an art derived from science. The problem with most cold calls is that they are mindless and lack conviction, like a golfer's swing who only plays a few times a year.

90 percent of "cold" calls are nebulous. You have no right calling that prospect. You are wasting *his* time (not yours, you are being paid to be inept). No wonder he screens you out. You deserve it. And that's the most common complaint from business development folks who are "cold" calling—they can't get their call through. They get their email deleted. They get their voicemail erased. They get screened out by the gatekeeper. You're a professional salesman, dammit! Act like one.

Golf doesn't teach character or humility, it reveals it. Fear is what sabotages most golf swings and what undermines most business development outreach efforts (phone call or otherwise). We're afraid of hitting a bad shot. We're afraid of sounding like a fool to the prospect because we haven't practiced enough or done our homework. If that's you, don't play and expect to be good or cold call and expect results.

20

ALEX BOGUSKY
ON NEW BUSINESS

The first time I heard Alex Bogusky's voice was in 1991. I was running Creative Search in Raleigh, North Carolina—a creative headhunting firm specializing in recruiting talent for regional creative agencies. He called me and declared that he wanted to build something special, an agency "that will ruin it for everyone" and that the only way for him to do it was to attract the "best rising talent" in the business. Alex referred to these relative unknowns as "mutts." And he needed my help to do it. He was just named Creative Director of the fledgling shop with fifteen employees in Miami and he was now empowered by Chuck Porter to act on this vision.

If I had a buck for every creative director who called me with this request, I could afford to spend the Fourth of July in The Hamptons. But, there was something in this guy's voice that was irresistible, like a force of nature. I bought it and devoted my commission-only time to helping Alex build his agency. At first, it was a challenging sell.

Hurricane Andrew hit Miami in 1992 and Tony Montana's city was not exactly the creative epicenter of the country to begin with. Alex was undeterred. Hurricane Andrew forced Alex and Chuck to reposition the agency. They would get away from being a "South Florida shop." They eschewed the typically lifeblood local accounts—tourism, real estate, hospitality. All that business was dead for the time being.

Instead, Alex pledged to follow his passion and chase smallish, but national outdoor enthusiast accounts, even if they were West Coast-based companies. He "lived" these brands, as did most of the staff at C&P. Creating great work for these outdoor brands enabled the agency to target hip, young demographic accounts—morphing eventually into the "kings of pop culture." It was a 10-year ascension to the throne. The account trail went like this:

Giro Helmets> Shimano> TRUTH> Mini> Burger King> Volkswagen> Microsoft

And along the way, I helped Alex recruit the best "mutts" in the country and moved them to the land of lox and bagels.

Alex delivered a keynote speech on new business at an *Adweek*-sponsored conference in New York City. The theme was "defying convention" and "breaking the rules."

Here are some quotes from the speech:

"The danger in our approach to business is we always look

for examples of who knows how to do it... We realized no one knows what the hell they are doing. And that was the real realization, that no one knows... and so then what do you do?"

"You have to take the time to also understand what turns you on about the business and that's one of the most important filters."

"Understand who you are in all this."

"The reason why (CP+B) didn't have to pitch was that we wound up unique. We made these ideas about what we think mattered in the industry, and they were distinct. And we changed our process."

"(New business pitches are) the time where we do our R&D. Where we think about where the industry is going. Where we think about new stories, where we're able to do it exactly the way we'd want to do it without a lot of interference."

"Your (agency model) is going to be unique. If it isn't really unique, it probably won't happen."

21

THE NEW AGENCY PITCH:
WHAT'S WORKING NOW

So you got a meeting. A prospect has agreed to meet with you or your agency has advanced in a pitch process. Great. Now what?

The trap is to plan the agenda around your agency's credentials. Don't fall in it. I've been on both sides of the table: as an agency search consultant for brand marketers and as a business development consultant for agencies. I've observed what entices clients to bite (the new meeting) and what causes them to fishtail away (the old way).

OLD WAY

- *This is who we are.* Riddled with clichés and pompous agency-speak.

- *This is what we do.* Puffed-up agency capabilities and service offerings.
- *This is how we work.* Trademarks, proprietary processes, secret sauces.
- *This is the proof (work & case studies).* Eyes begin to glaze over by the second case study.
- *"Ok, enough about us, let's talk about you..."* The client is checking their watch and phone by now.

The best and most effective meetings I've been a part of in the past few years (on both sides of the table) begin something like this: The agency leader puts a jump drive on the conference table in front of the client and says, "Here are our credentials, if we have time and you are interested, we can take you through them. But, we're here to discuss your brand and your business and learn more about your challenges." Then the meeting proceeds something like this:

NEW WAY

- *This is who you are (brand video, brand book, or manifesto).* The best meetings begin by making an emotional connection with the client. They think, "Wow, they get us."
- *This is why we like you (missions aligned).* Demonstrate passion, don't talk about it.
- *This is your customer (and they are us).* Don't pitch prospects you don't believe in.

- *These are your challenges (truthful).* Address the toughest challenges, the brutal facts.
- *These are our ideas for you.* Business ideas, marketing ideas not necessarily spec creative.
- *"Oh, you want to know more about us? Sure..."* Now you've got their attention as they fumble around for the jump drive.

Now they want to see your case studies to see if you have experience in successfully executing similar business/marketing ideas for other clients. Now you have a chance to win their business.

22

THE NEW AGENCY WEBSITE:
WHAT'S WORKING NOW

So this is the digital age. You are not just an ad agency anymore. You are now a hybrid, Tradigital, media agnostic, nimble, agile, curating creator of commercial content. Good for you. Why does your website still look like an ad agency's?

It's no great insight that your company's single most important piece of identity is your website. It's where you send prospects, clients, search consultants, headhunters and potential employees to learn more about you and what you do. It's where Google sends anyone who searches your name. It's probably the most important piece of communication you will ever create. I spend most of my waking life looking at these things. Why am I mostly underwhelmed?

Recently, an old friend called to say he was re-doing his agency's site and asked if I had any tips. This man, mind you, has one of the most startling imaginations of any creative I have worked with in my thirty-five years in advertising. In short, a great new site takes a great imagination. So he's off to a good start. Make sure you appoint your most imaginative minds to your new site. The old site was a "business tool." The new site is much more than that. It's your digital persona.

The trap is to talk to yourselves. Don't fall in it. I've looked at agency sites from every possible angle: with clients as a search consultant, as a headhunter, as a recruit and as a biz dev person. I've observed what causes your targets to keep clicking (the new site) or opt out (the old site).

OLD SITE

- *Themeless.* No connection of your positioning to any mission, purpose or specialty.
- *Words.* "About us"...riddled with clichés and pompous agency-speak.
- *Pictures.* Ads, headshots, office space, ping-pong tables, posers posing for "candid" photos.
- *Case studies.* "When Acme Corporation came to us, boy were they up shit's creek. We saved the day with our trademarked processes, brilliant insights (and mediocre) creative, and here's how..."
- *Bios.* "Joe has won every imaginable award on the planet. He loves dogs and look how handsome he is."
- *TV spots.* Usually the only moving thing on the site besides

that unsettling download onto the landing page.
- *CTA.* "What are you waiting for? Fill out this generic form below."

NEW SITE

- *Theme.* The site makes an immediate statement and emotional connection to what the agency brand stands for
- *Video.* The connection is made through a short agency video that connects the agency's positioning with the core values of your targets. This is the first thing that comes up front & center on your landing page.
- *Infographics.* The most effective way to explain who you are, what you do and why you do it. "The agency in 60 seconds" is a better link to these than "About us."
- *Creative showcase.* Don't "let the work speak for itself."
- *Case studies.* 1 minute videos or infographic, beautifully designed.
- *Bios.* 30-second videos. A great creative opportunity.
- *CTA.* Again, a video. Close me; in a brilliantly unique and entertaining way.

Now they want to learn more about you. People don't read websites until they want to buy. They look. They watch. They share. This is the digital age, lest we forget.

23

THE ALL-VIDEO RFP:
IT'S ABOUT TIME

So your agency just spent about 200 hours frantically copying & pasting a written RFP response which you submitted a few minutes before the deadline. We all know the drill: assign sections of the response to a handful of senior managers and pour the ingredients into your RFP template. Then package it in a nifty custom binder and FedEx it off to the search consultant or Client.

Then what happens?

Unfortunately, not much. I was quite surprised when I started running agency reviews five years ago how little of the written responses were actually read in the initial stage of the process. What I learned was that the voluminous agency tomes (many exceeding 100 pages) were perfunctorily glanced at, thumbed through or ignored entirely.

A video component has been a part of the RFP process for about twenty-five years. The first one I ever saw came from Boston-based Pile & Company around 2001 and it asked for a short agency "culture video." Then a few years later, it evolved into a request for a five- to ten-minute minute video of the agency team that would work on the account having a round-table discussion about the opportunity. I always incorporated the latter into my RFP's when managing a review.

But, a funny thing happened on the way to the forum. My clients were ONLY watching the videos and when impressed, they requested to look at the creative work. They ignored the written responses. Instead, they would simply ask me some of the key questions like, "how many employees?" and "where are they based?" and "do they have experience in our category?" And, of course, "where did they come out on their cost proposal?" They didn't read the written response until we boarded a plane to visit a semi-finalist agency!

This got me thinking...the video format allowed for break-through creativity and opportunities to make emotional connections with the client. It gave challenger agencies the chance to outhustle the big boys. The best ones entertained, educated and inspired. AND they saved everybody a ton of time. What if the RFP called for video response entirely?

I just finished my tenth ALL-video RFP review. We asked the basic twelve or so questions to be addressed upfront (employees, mission, process, etc.). And then we asked to meet the team. And then we gave them creative license to riff however they wanted: "Show us what you're all about…"

Most of the videos came in at 10-12 minutes in duration, and were shot with a GoPro camera. The good ones made us laugh or cry or get goosebumps (the best ones, all three). With ten courageous and innovative marketing clients, I think we revolutionized the Agency Review process.

It's not about saving trees…it's about saving time.

24

THE METER IS RUNNING: WHY ACCOUNTS ARE ALWAYS IN REVIEW

We've all sat helplessly as our taxicab wades glacially through heavy traffic—one eye on the meter. There's nothing worse than the feeling of paying good money to go nowhere. This is the main reason why there are so insufferably many ad account reviews these days. Clients need results now—this week (retailers), this quarter (publicly traded companies) or even today (Cellular phone companies). They feel like we do in that cab.

Many of them cannot afford to wait out a quarter or two. It's not just the clients' jobs on the line. It's their CEO's, as well. We're truly living in a "win now, or go home" world. That's the reality. You produce results now or you're toast—and sometimes, you're toast either way.

Client job turnover is often directly correlative to client/

agency turnover. It shouldn't surprise anyone that a new CMO will probably look for a new agency. I've read that the average CMO job tenure hovers at around twenty months. As Don Corleone said, "This is the life we have chosen." It just moves a whole LOT faster now. It's funny that some pitch consultants complain about this doom loop, exaggerating market conditions along the way. I find it ironic since their niche exists primarily on the pretext of volatility.

I think it's a good thing. Darwinism. Performance-based agency compensation. Incentive-based employee compensation. All this will make our industry hungrier and better. We will earn what we're worth. This is the foundation of Capitalism (which may be just as fractured as the ad industry these days). But the agencies that whine about it usually lose the business, while the ones who embrace it, win it.

Accounts move away quickly for a multitude of reasons. Among them:

- The agency is not providing the thought leadership they promised as "specialists" in their industry.
- The agency swooped in with a crackerjack pitch team that the client hardly ever saw again... until compensation time.
- The agency is so busy pitching/soliciting new business that they neglect the client.
- Employee turnover at the agency (formerly the biggest reason of all).
- Mediocre creative work.

- Lack of a service mentality at the agency—just plain bad customer service (it starts at the switchboard).
- CMO turnover (duh).
- Unforeseen business turnover (banks & hospitals get bought, merged, etc.).
- Sluggish sales (not always the agency's fault, but almost always the agency's blame).
- The client simply falls out of love, someone prettier comes along who is doing sexier work—you lose the beauty contest.
- The pigs at corporate suck up all the marketing dollars for their bonuses—cut marketing budgets.
- A new business professional at another agency steals the account by building a meaningful business relationship and seizes the moment (that moment you dropped the ball on a key deliverable).
- Change for change's sake.

It's also ironic that so many agencies chestbeat about how they are "change agents," but they find it difficult to understand when their own clients' brands need a change, a fresh perspective, new eyes and ears. And, above all, a new voice.

This is advertising. There's no crying in advertising.

There are only two guarantees:

1. Accounts come and go.
2. People come and go.

25

WHAT YOU CAN LEARN
FROM CHARLES DARWIN

Charles Darwin may very well be the most quoted person of the past 150 years. So, what's the big deal? More important to us, how does he apply to creativity? At the heart of Darwin's theory was the idea that each species adapts to its environment. From this process of change, new species arise. This theory has relevance to agencies and marketers seeking to spread their message in a changing marketplace; let's call this the marketing evolution.

While on a journey aboard the HMS Beagle (now that would be a cool name for an ad agency), Darwin observed that every island of the Galapagos had its own type of finch. While these birds were closely familiar, they differed in subtle, but significant ways. This holds truth when a marketer attempts to distribute their message across various platforms.

Darwin theorized that organisms best suited to their environment had a greater chance of survival and reproduction. They passed along their key survival characteristics to their offspring

Today's agencies and marketers that distribute brand messages through multiple platforms are prone to Darwin's theory. Competing for attention in each channel, key "survival traits" are necessary for optimal success. While "content is king," both context and relevance matter—if neglected, the message can disappear and the brand faces extinction.

Here are five theories Darwn outlined in *On the Origin of Species,* and how they apply to brand content marketing evolution:

1. *Evolution.* "While species come and go through time, they change during their existence"—Branding and marketing aren't new. Brands have always relied on content to survive. But, content has evolved over time. It started as stories told around the campfire to teach and entertain family and friends. Make sure your brand's content can evolve with the times. The best way to accomplish this is to use stories about your business. Storybuilding (I don't like the cliché "storytelling") is how people will remember your brand.

2. *Common Descent.* "While organisms descend from one or

more common ancestors, they diversify from the original stock"—Diversify your content! Use various techniques—text, photos, infographics, videos, etc... Don't be a one-trick pony.

3. *Species Multiply.* "Diversification involves the population of one species changing until they become two distinct species"—Allow your brand message to multiply. Create subsequent content around your core brand and products. Your brand will take on exponential lives.

4. *Gradualism.* "New species don't occur suddenly. Rather evolutionary alterations happen with small incremental changes inside populations"—Content distribution is not effective simply by getting it out there. Adapt it powerfully for each platform and channel. Drip it.

5. *Natural Selection.* "Evolution occurs due to differences between individual species' therefore some variations provide improved chances for survival"—Just as natural selection affects species competition, each piece of marketing content struggles for attention. Success is not about mass volume attention but about the most relevant content to the most relevant consumer. Create content that ensures that. Successful messages survive.

26

WHAT YOU CAN LEARN FROM HOLDEN CAULFIELD: MY HOMAGE TO J.D. SALINGER

While sauntering aimlessly up Madison Avenue one tepid autumnal afternoon, I could not help but think of my favorite protagonist and what he might think of the advertising industry. Holden Caulfield, the thinly veiled autobiographical character created for *Catcher in the Rye* would have made a terrific copywriter. If you want to know the truth, he also would have made a great brand marketer, and I'm not kidding. I know what I'm talking about.

While strolling amidst these phony baloney ad execs at lunchtime, you think of all the phony messages and claims brands make and have always made: "Stronger than Dirt," "Save Money, Live Better" (the poor Simpletons who believe that...), "Open Happiness" (me and Holden never much trusted happiness)...yeah sure. What a bastion of disingenuity this advertising game is.

If there's one thing I hate, it's commercials. Don't even mention them to me. The actors are phony. Holden would have written commercials that didn't rely on an actor's talent. He would made the product and the benefit the stars. He would have written honest commercials, like "We know you hate shaving, it's a chore and time-consuming and boring. Our razor is not going to save your life, or make shaving more fun, or make you more handsome so you can have more silly girlfriends (most girls are so dumb and all)...but our razor is made right here in America and if you buy it, you have a conscience and here's why...." At least the company would communicate a mission and make a real emotional connection; not just an appeal to narcissism.

Holden was authentic, unlike most advertising today. It's faked, like it's a movie. Is there anything less authentic than this new "hidden camera" trick? However immature, Holden was true to his conscience.

If you really want to hear about real creative advertising, here's what Holden might tell you, and he's not kidding:

1. Be honest about your brand
2. Be authentic
3. Stop trying to impress everyone (know your target)
4. Have a mission (beyond selling stuff)
5. Communicate your mission with a humble swagger

27

BLOW UP YOUR AGENCY
IN FIVE EASY PIECES

Talk is cheap, as Keith Richards taught us. It's time to stop analyzing this. Analysis is paralysis. It's time to act. You love the smell of napalm in the morning? So, let's make some:

1. *Fire that Abusive, Adulterous Client.* You know who they are. Everyone has one. They think they own you. You let them. They will kill you with a toothpick. Whack them first. It will be better for morale in the long run. You may have to lay off some enablers, but sometimes it's good to cut out the dead wood. This client threatens you. They run you through flaming hoops. They seek creative sex on the side. Do you really want their money? Who's the whore—them or you? Make it them. Marry Madonna, not the whore.

2. *Turn the Firing Into a Press Release.* Crispin has done this well. They fire the client citing "Creative Differences" and take the story to the Trade Press. They make it clear that they have experience in the category and they are now actively seeking a new partner that would like to exploit that experience to their advantage. Crispin did this quite well when they "fired" Nike and were subsequently hired by UnderArmor. What is more compelling than a "man bites dog" story?

3. *It's the Creative, Stupid.* Strategy is good. So is Service. And, it's awfully nice of you have an Understanding of their Business. Digital fluency... hey, great. Clients consider all these things to be included in the price of playing poker; mere table stakes. These are checked boxes and all are purely a means to an end. That end is Creative Execution. You've invested millions in cool office space, facilities, processes and technologies—but, your creative is just fair, at best. If you can't sell your agency with your work, then good luck selling it with all this other stuff. Above all else, clients seek agencies for their *creative* communications. Do great work and new business will come to you. You want Inbound Marketing? Then do great work. How? It starts at the top.

4. *Hire Leaders, Fire Followers.* What's at the top filters down. If you are retaining leadership (Creative or otherwise) simply to maintain existing business by not making waves or

rocking the boat, then you will never grow. You will continue running on the treadmill. You will only get phone sex and not the real thing. Your coffee will be decaf. Sorry, but to grow, you have to risk rocking the boat. Your good clients will recognize and respect that you are really acting in their best interests by changing. You are upping the ante. You are improving your game. Stand still, and you will die a slow death.

5. *Be Decisive, Don't Look Back.* Put a stake in the ground. What is your agency's value proposition? How do you create a point of differentiation? If you create nothing else—create that. Make that POD ownable. Then rebrand yourself accordingly. Make it simple and universally understandable. If you have to explain who you are in more than 20 seconds...then BLOW IT UP. It won't work anymore. The rate of change around you is so rapid. you'll get whiplash.

28

ADVERTISING IN THE GARDEN OF GOOD AND EVIL: HOW AGENCIES AND BRANDS FEED EACH FRENZY

A curious and somewhat troubling inertia is pressing upon the advertising industry. It represents a conflict as primary and epic as Milton's *Paradise Lost* and *Genesis 3*. The conflict is, essentially and literally, Good v. Evil.

In the beginning, God didn't really want us to know the difference. He omnisciently wanted to wait on that one for another 4,000 years or so. But, the low-hanging forbidden fruit dangled seductively from a particular tree. That sacred, yet grasp-able tree, according to the Bible, was The Tree of the Knowledge of Good & Evil. Its nectar produced Godliness, Godly knowledge. The knowledge of... good and evil.

We look to our institutions for leadership and to provide valuable knowledge. We award degrees for levels of knowledge—various degrees in various degrees. Institutions: universities, churches, hospitals, banks and the like, don't *reflect* society. It is their purpose to *lead* it. They must remain as constant as the northern star. They are our true compass. Institutions tell us things and we believe them, sometimes as gospel. If our governing institutions tell us that Osama bin Laden was assassinated, for example, we believe them. Even if a body or photographic evidence does not exist. We believe them. They lead us and they don't stoop to our level by providing proof. (As an aside, did you ever notice that an assassin has two asses?)

This is also the way other institutions, like churches, work. They insist that God is a mystery. There's no physical proof of a god. There doesn't need to be. Oh, I know there were a bunch of miracles in Italy—and a shroud exists. But, religious institutions demand that we maintain this sort of blind faith.

Medical institutions claim there is no known cure for cancer. We believe them. Academic institutions deem what is and isn't valid and useful knowledge by their curricula—nobody questions that. It's mono-cultural and flat—this is this and it is what it is: your education. Now go out into the world and make something of yourself. You are cast east of Eden.

Advertising agency people don't consider their industry institutional. They're too maverick, too iconoclastic. Conversely, people outside of our industry view us as if we *are* an institution. They talk about us as if we're really important—like we actually do have an institutional effect on society. Or at least they blame us when we are negligent in our messaging. Our clients get class-action lawsuits when the beef we advertise as real beef is just 38 percent, uh, beef. Some women blame anorexia on advertising. Yes, we have that kind of institutional control over society. This is how we deal with it: we *reflect* society instead of *leading* it. We insist on proof. We claim knowledge—intimate and insightful knowledge. We reflect society—we take it and give it right back.

Except this is how it all really works in advertising: some brilliant creative mind sifts through all the crap from research and focus groups (anything can be proven with statistics and then immediately disproved, as well) and creates something somewhat magical—an idea. Then everyone goes back and rewrites revisionist history—building a bulletproof case for that idea that even Columbo couldn't crack.

How else could today's advertising be so violent? I got whiplash watching the Super Bowl spots. Has advertising ever been so gruesome? How about the new Alec Baldwin ads for New Era caps? That's supposed to be funny? A Red Sox fan getting punched in the face by a Yankee fan is funny? We are reflecting society—not leading it. Agencies would like us to believe that they tested a modern Three Stooges routine with the target dummies in focus groups and they came out with the insightful knowledge that Betty White and Abe Vigoda getting smacked down into the mud is funny.

Our knowledge tells us that violence is funny. Unexpected violence is REALLY funny. Shame on us for reflecting society in such a self-serving and evil way. No wonder some women blame us for anorexia. How do brands allow it? I liked us better when we airbrushed naked women on the ice cubes in liquor ads. When sex and violence was subliminal, it was cool. It's just way too obvious today.

On the other side of the fulcrum of this inertia is the trendy way brands and agencies are hopping on the "cause" and "purpose" bandwagon. I mean, even Gucci is into cause marketing. Give me a break. How many alligators do they kill per year? I suppose their customers want to feel good about themselves despite their conspicuously narcissistic species-endangering consumption. And I suppose brands also realize how disingenuous and mindless their advertising appears so they may be trying to overcompensate with cause initiatives. But even those initiatives reflect society rather than lead it. Agencies always brag that they can change or motivate certain behaviors. What if they actually did this for good instead of evil?

Let's look at the Volkswagen brand as an example:

A few years ago, VW hired Crispin and unleashed a new mascot upon the great autobahn of life. He was named, "FAST." I can only imagine how this happened—Crispin told VW that they understood how to connect with young people (the Truth campaign) and they understood how to sell them cars (Mini). They probably told them there was a huge, untapped youth market for VW and they knew just how to suck them in. Young people want to go FAST.

Hence, this creepy mascot named FAST was born. They probably went into focus groups and came out with the precious insight that young people like to drive fast. This is neither responsible nor institutional. It reflects what's bad in society instead of leading it. Maybe it's just me, but I can't imagine a greater disconnect than that of the Volkswagen brand and the concept of FAST.

Fast forward to the 2011 Super Bowl. A wonderful and humane Volkswagen commercial produced by Deutsch entitled "Darth Vader" (who ironically looks strikingly similar to the FAST mascot). It made VW owners and prospective owners feel good about their car and themselves. So how does that lead society? Just the other day I was driving on a crowded midtown street. Suddenly, a DPW truck filling a pothole blocked my lane. I had 20 yards to stop or change lanes. In my rearview mirror I saw the driver of the car in the left lane motioning me to cut in front of him. He slowed down and allowed me to change lanes without incident. It was a Volkswagen. He didn't care about FAST. He just wanted to do good.

Do you think it's possible that VW's advertising might have influenced that random act of good? I wonder.

29

THE SEVEN DEADLY SINS
OF ADVERTISING: WEAKNESS IN
THE SHADOWS OF STRENGTH

One of my all-time favorite quotes comes from the great Irish playwright and poet, Oscar Wilde, "I can resist everything except temptation" (scripted from the play, *Lady Windermere's Fan*). We're all human—each one of us prone to temptation and the foibles of this earthly experience.

Ad agencies are merely the sum total of the humans that inhabit their halls. 90 percent of an agency's inventory disappears nightly via the elevator. When the sum of the parts of that human total exceeds the whole, a creative agency is in a position to catch lightning in a bottle—to be magical. It is this elusive magical elixir that seduces agencies, tempting them to succumb to their weaknesses.

I ran a reference check on an executive creative director. While speaking to their former account planning partner, I

asked him what this particular candidate's strengths were—
and then I asked about their weaknesses. The planner's answer
was enlightening (that is his job, after all): "his weaknesses are
merely shadows of his strengths." That was a simple, but seis-
mic insight.

Our weaknesses are merely shadows of our strengths.
This applies to all people-first companies, like creative agencies. Human nature is fairly predictable. Chaucer taught us
through his knight in *Canterbury Tales* that there is"nothing
new under the sun" (turns out that even this message wasn't
new as it appeared first in *Ecclesiastes 1:9*).

So what can we learn from our weaknesses in trying to
grow our creative agencies? What temptations will most
likely lead to demise? What sins do we commit that may ultimately lead to our death?

THE SEVEN DEADLY SINS OF ADVERTISING

PRIDE—*the excessive belief in our abilities.* There's a fine
line between confidence and pride. We often demand that
our people "take pride" in their work. This is a strength that
is shadowed by weakness. An example is the ridiculously
self-important and self-promotional case studies that appear
on agency websites. Not only do they reveal strategies to our
clients' competitors, they often make it seem like our clients
couldn't succeed without us. We make it seem like we have
some special secret sauce that other agencies don't. Another

example is the way we put silly TM's on processes that are pretty much self-evident and use fancy words when simple ones will do. Agencies don't appear humble, even if their people are. It's like our profession seduces us all, as if we think we're on Mad Men, or something. Makes me want to get out of business development.

ENVY—*the desire for others' status or abilities.* Is this a wannabe business, or what? I mean one scrappy little designer, Alex Bogusky, takes an eighteen-person shop and makes them a global creative superpower and everyone thinks they can do it. I guess anything is possible, but it took Alex ten years to become an overnight sensation. And it required tireless devotion and a deal with the devil at the crossroads with Robert Johnson for that to happen.

Agencies should focus on what they can be the best at in their region and pursue that. They should talk to their core targets and invite others to listen in. They should have a simple, humble mission and stick to it. We're an envious industry— when there's a big public account review and we're not in it, we secretly hope that NOBODY wins it. It reminds me of being a college basketball coach. Those guys open *USA Today* in the morning and hope they see that everyone lost the night before.

GLUTTONY—or in the old days when language was elegant, profligacy. *The inordinate desire to consume more than that which one requires.* McGarry/Bowen comes to mind. Sure they're on a roll now. But, just wait—pride and gluttony goeth before the fall. How is it possible to win all that business and service it diligently? But, let's scale this sin down to the local and regional level. So many agencies get caught up in new business "activity." They call it a "numbers game." Tell that to your new client—that they were a number, welcome aboard.

Guys sometimes call me and say that they can't do their job properly because they're "in four pitches this month." What? It's hard enough to pitch ONE properly. Not to mention pitch one and keep your current clients happy at the same time. We wind up just hoping that the line coming in the front door is slightly longer than the line going out. Gluttony also destroyed agency compensation models. It got so bad that clients hired consultants to monitor their agency's financial efficiency. And it spurned entire gumshoe departments known as "procurement."

LUST—*inordinate craving for pleasures of the body.* Why did you choose advertising as a profession? Let's face it—the babes are hotter than anywhere else. Admit it, you horndog. Maybe the bigger question is why do all the hot babes get hired by agencies? I'm sure I'll get hateful comments branding me as a sexist or a pig (or maybe both, if I'm lucky). Whatever. Chicks dig the long ball.

ANGER—also known as wrath, *is manifested when an agency spurns love and opts instead for fury.* You can spot an angry agency pretty easily. Doesn't matter how big or small it is. The receptionist sets a condescending tone. Your parking is not validated. The pizza's cold. People appear stressed, overworked and challenged to keep up with their tasks. The understaffed team hasn't received bonuses in years. A few people make all the money (usually fat, white guys in the suburbs). Only a few opinions are valued. Anger can also often be subtle and passive-aggressive, more difficult to recognize and decipher. Haters appear to be lovers. Lovers appear to be haters. Nobody knows whom not to trust. We've all worked somewhere like this at some point.

GREED—or, Avarice. *The desire for material wealth or gain while ignoring the spirit.* Don't get me wrong—material wealth is fine. We're all in this to make money. It's the ignoring the spirit part that is deadly. So, whatever happened to *Pro bono?* It's all but gone from the industry. And when we do it, it STILL comes with an ulterior motive: "If we can't win awards on *Pro bono,* then why do it?" Huh? Think about the hypocrisy of that statement.

How many agencies are truly integrated into their communities? How many align themselves with institutions, educational and otherwise? You always hear the bullshit line, "the soul of the agency"—and then you look at the client list and they sell booze and fast food. Don't get me wrong; booze and fast food are legal and part of the great capitalist dream. But booze is the third leading cause of death in America and poor diet is not far behind.

We often get paid to help people kill themselves. We glorify the temptation. That's our craft. So, at least be penitent on your way to the bank. The most successful people I've known in this business treated their career and their agency as if it were a vocation—not a profession or a mint.

SLOTH—I love that word. It just sounds so much like it is, almost onomatopoeia. *The avoidance of physical work.* Agencies expect to "get to the next level" (they rarely define what that actually means) as if they are simply entitled to it. Everyone wants to succeed, but few are willing to prepare for success. Bobby Knight said that. He probably stole it from Chaucer, who probably stole it from one of the Prophets.

I've noticed that there's a high correlation to agencies that talk about "getting to the next level" all the time and ones that are barren and desolate at 5:15 p.m. (unless it's freelancers in the creative department fixing the mistakes and revisions of the FTEs). And it's funny when the FTEs complain about how hard their job is. It's friggin' advertising! Go dig ditches for a week, then come back and explain how difficult your agency job is. Fat, drunk and strategic is no way to go through life, you horndog.

30

HIDE THE BUDDHA

We have our principles...
and if you don't like those, we have others.

New Business people have plenty of pitch war stories. There's the urban legend about how the Aflac Duck came into existence, supposedly on the elevator with the client after the pitch creative failed in the formal presentation. Then there's the notorious story how BBDO stole the Cingular Wireless account from what was then known as WestWayne (now monikered 22squared) after the selection committee chose the Atlanta independents. Maybe the juiciest of all was the Wal-Mart pitch led by Julie Roehm, choosing Draft/FCB, but then having to re-review the account following tales of impropriety, lust and betrayal (ultimately settling in at The Martin Agency). If you're in New Business, you have a war story—or several.

My favorite centers upon a character named Tim Bayless. I'm fortunate to have worked with many magical personalities in my *Gump-ish* life: Jim Valvano, Rick Pitino, John Calipari, Lee Clow, Bogusky, David Lubars, Andrew Robertson, Richard Ward, Doug MacMillan (The Connells), among others. Bayless had as much magic in him as any of them. Tim started an agency on his kitchen table in Atlanta in 1994 and proceeded to build one of the hottest shops in the country within five years. He recruited the writer (Jerry Cronin) that created the most famous Nike and ESPN work (at a time when getting talented creatives to move to Atlanta was harder than getting the Olympics to come to town). In his sixth year, he sold the agency to Omnicom. Think about that... a guy with not much else besides gumption, starts an agency alone on his kitchen table and six years later sells it to Omnicom for millions. That's magic.

About twenty years ago, I was helping Tim with business development. We had just lost the agency's cornerstone Church's Chicken account. So Tim ordered me to "call every chicken company in America and tell them we're available." We didn't have to look very far. Atlanta (and the regional Southeast) is the fried chicken capital of the world. Chick-fil-A became an obsessive target. I badgered their marketing people for weeks. Told them "nobody will like this *cow* stuff you're doing." And "The Richards Group is the *Dead Poet's Society*" and desperately, "Why is such a civic-minded, community-based company like yours taking jobs and business to Dallas?" Finally, I struck a nerve and one Friday, they emailed me and agreed to meet with us "soon."

That same Friday we also received an RFP from Van Gogh Vodka. The RFP arrived in a box with dozens of mini airplane bottle-sized samples of flavored vodkas—chocolate vodka, raspberry vodka, et al. along with all the mixing accouterments—all these flavors at a time when flavored vodkas were relatively new. So, at around four pm that afternoon, I sent an email to all agency personnel that we would be "doing research" on these flavored vodkas for the RFP in the main conference room and all were invited.

Within five minutes, the conference room was teeming with everyone from our controller (boy did HE need a drink, trying to balance Bayless' books) to our building's janitor. It was a real mix-off, concocting potions previously unimaginable. And we were catching a bit of a buzz.

At one point amidst all this mixology, our receptionist came into the conference room to alert me of a phone call. I retreated to my office and took the call. It was the CMO from Chick-fil-A. He said he wanted to come by the agency to meet with us. "Awesome!" I exclaimed, "When would you guys like to come, what day works best for you?"

"Uh, we're in Midtown NOW and would like to come by the agency on our way back to the office." Their "office campus" is near the Atlanta airport. "I'm with Mr. Cathy (S. Truett Cathy, CEO and famously devout Christian) and he'd like to meet you, too."

"Nanananowww?" I stammered.

"Yes, now. We'll be there in ten minutes."

"Sounds great. See you then. Do you know how to get here?"

I never heard their answer because I was already hustling over to Tim's office. In the center of the agency, in the "public area" of BaylessCronin sat a large Buddha statue and fountain.

The Buddha symbolized all the agency's manufactured new age values: peace, tranquility, spirituality, and mysticism. It anchored the most visible and central spot in our space. It was the star of the show, the belle of the ball. The flowing fountain was symbolic of the lifestream of the agency and our values.

I barged into Tim's office.

"I've got good news and I've got bad news."

Tim never wanted to know bad news.

"What's the good news?"

"Chick-fil-A is coming to the agency to meet with us," I blurted.

"Awesome. What could be the bad news?" Tim cackled.

"They'll be here in eight minutes. The CMO and S. Truett Cathy. What are we going to do? Everyone's getting hammered in the conference room."

Tim took all of five seconds to respond. It was the single most brilliant answer to a question I've heard in my entire ad agency life.

"Quick, hide the buddha."

The Agency

NEW BUSINESS PRIMER

31

CHOOSE FIVE COMPANIES
THAT MAKE BUSINESS SENSE

Let's start backwards (always a good idea in new business).

First, go to your local stationery store and buy five large three-ring binders. Do not buy them at Wal-Mart or any other chain. They will not work. It is bad karma. You are an entrepreneur and the core of your new business program must be entrepreneurial in every sense. These binders will sit on your credenza until you feel a current account is vulnerable.

That may take a day, a week or a month. It will not take longer than that. What should go into these binders? Start with this checklist:

- History overview of company
- Sales and stock performance
- Products and services

- Who's who
- CEO
- Bios on all players (not just Marketing)
- Who at your agency knows whom there?
- Structure of marketing department
- Former agency relationship
- Recent news
- Current challenges, outlook
- Website
- *Forbes, WSJ, Fortune* (alerts)
- Advertising/marketing
- *Redbook* or *Brandweek* listing for the company
- Agency relationship
- *Redbook* or *Adweek* listing(s) on agencies
- Recent press: *Adweek, Ad Age*
- Spending
- Apparent marketing strategy
- Overview on current campaign
- Examples of advertising
- Target audience(s)/consumer(s)
- Tactics used
- Industry overview
- Trends outlook
- Subscribe to trade publications
- Key competitors
- Brief overview of each competitor

Now comes the hard part. Which five companies become your primary new business targets? First and foremost, your top prospects should make common business sense. This does not always mean that you have matchy-matchy relevant experience in their category. This is a shortcut to the truth imposed upon agencies by search consultants and new business seminars. Of course, relevant experience is helpful, but there are other equally important criteria that should guide the decision.

Pretend you are a college basketball coach and you are recruiting a starting five. You won't win with five point guards or five centers. Strive for a balance. Recruit these companies as you would players. You are recruiting your agency client roster.

Some criteria to consider:

1. *Geography*. A 180-mile radius from your address is not a bad start. Although some agencies like Crispin were forced to expand their geography (Hurricane Andrew 1992). With the amount of effort and study required to devote to this program, I recommend keeping all five prospects within a convenient commute to the prospect.

2. *Industry Experience*. This either really works or it really doesn't. More and more clients are anxious to break out of their category and become, as David Lubars says, "a category of one." Study the history of the CMO: a category "follower" or a "trailblazer?" Don't assume category experience is always a plus.

3. *Demographic.* This was the key to Crispin's success. They made a decision to break out of the typical South Florida agency mindset (real estate, hospitality, tourism) and follow their passions. Today they are known as pop-culturalists, but it all started with chasing prospects for which they "had a passion for their products." That morphed into the agency that "knows how to talk to young consumers."

   The logic trail: "chase the brands we like," become known as the agency that speaks to enthusiasts (those brands not so coincidentally had *young* enthusiasts), become known as the agency that knows how to talk to young consumers. RESULT: Masters of pop cultural language. Sounds easy? It took ten years.

4. *Psychographic.* What triggers do you ignite for your current clients? What do they sell? Not products or services—are they affluent? Blue collar? Are they low-interest purchases? Big-ticket purchases? One-time purchases? Daily transactions? E-commerce? Moms? Single gay dads?

5. *Purpose.* GSD&M is doing a great job selling "Purpose-based Branding." Want to know what it is? Google it and Roy Spence. Buy the book on Amazon.

Criteria to dismiss: any criteria that is self-serving.

1. Creative opportunity (you can win awards on the local tattoo parlor, like Jelly Helm did).
2. Case study opportunity.
3. It's a "dream account."
4. You want to fill a vacant category on your roster.
5. They "need your help."

Form a new business "council" of your most ambitious people (not your most "senior"). Ask for input. Make a decision on five prospects. Put a stake in the ground. Assign a team to each "account." *Get smart* on your prospects' business.

32

STUDY THEIR BUSINESS, CATEGORIES, INDUSTRIES, AND MARKET EFFECTS

It's funny how everybody at the agency wants to help with New Business, until you ask. Then they seem to go dark into the black hole of account emergencies/personal dilemmas/ health problems/pet responsibilities/kid's soccer games/ deaths in the family, etc. Then, when they're laid off due to an account loss attributed to a new CMO (just a matter of time) they run to Agency Spy and dish the dirt on how lame the agency is.

It's critical to establish an inclusive new business culture. Donny Deutsch once said that new business is a *religion* within the agency. Like Mass (I doubt Donny ever went to Mass), it's good to attend a weekly "service." Some agencies do this first thing every Monday morning. This is a good idea. To paraphrase *Field of Dreams,* if you put out free food, they will come. Krispy Kreme and chicken biscuits usually work.

Recruit a new business "war council" of your most ambitious people. Make sure all disciplines are represented, including administrative, financial, IT and even custodial (you'll be surprised what you'll learn from them). Invite your most *ambitious* people, not necessarily your "best and brightest." Invite the rebels and iconoclasts. They have a great new business mentality.

Don't make this Monday morning meeting a "dashboard report." Make it a lively discussion forum. Encourage new outreach ideas. Reward those ideas when they secure a meeting or drive an inquiry. Once a year, take this group offsite for inspiration. Bring in a New Business speaker/specialist.

Okay. You've got your top five prospects and three-ring binders. You have your new business council (give it a name—brand it within the agency, have fun with it but don't be a cornball). Now assign a team to each top-five prospect "account." It's their responsibility to fill the binders. It's their responsibility to formulate an educated POV on the prospect, their business, category, market effects, industry trends, etc.

I crack up when agencies rush to these ornate but makeshift "war rooms" once they get in a pitch. And they think clients fall for it—like they can learn enough in three weeks to form a credible POV on their business. Clients are smirking behind their back.

33

OUTREACH

Create an outreach program that is consistent,
polite, non-threatening and professional.

If you haven't heard the news, traditional outreach methods for agency business development have recently gone out of vogue. Like traditional advertising, they're out. How uncool to have an agency "book" or "reel." How uncool to call a prospect and try to have an actual conversation. And Heaven forbid we invite the prospect to breakfast or lunch or over to the agency for a beer.

There's a new way of communicating with our prospects, and it's totally sterile, fail-proof and guaranteed to grow your agency—you just tweet prospects to your blog and they become instant qualified leads. If you have narrowed your specialty offering to the point of banality—"we're the round hole for your round peg"—then new business just comes to you. Just tweet, blog and win. Sounds like a promotion. Bonus points if you write a book proving how smart you are—like Joey Reiman.

How jejune. I believe people do business with people. Most of the business I've ever seen move is the result of relationships. This is not about chumming for numberless prospects. It's about taking your agency's new business fate into its own hands; not waiting for someone to hit your blog. Do the social media *jagoff* (must be said with a Chicago accent) with the rest of your prospect list. This is about your top five prospects.

If you were a college basketball coach recruiting players—you would not have the same outreach program for your thirtieth rated recruit as you would your top five recruits. You've GOT to get one of those. So you spend more time, energy, creativity and passion recruiting them. Treat your top five prospects differently. They deserve 80 percent of your attention. In the meantime—you'll get RFPs, get referrals and have the same crappy accounts SEEK YOU OUT. You'll win some of those. But this is about building a strategic plan for the growth of your agency, and maintaining a consistent and creative dialogue with your prospects.

Let's start with the premise that you're a creative agency. If not, stop reading here. What do clients really want? Great creative. That's what makes them stars. They can leverage great creative with their CEO or to enhance their careers. Yes, they all talk about integration, ROI, service, planning, measurement, digital, social, yada yada. But ALL those things assume a great creative idea.

Creative is the end to all those means. You can call it content, ideation, or whatever you want. I still call it "creative." It's a noun, not an adjective. You have to ascribe to the theory that great creative EQUALS effectiveness. At BBDO, they like to talk about a study conducted by Millward Brown that award-winning work is 2,000 times more likely to be effective than other work. That's Millward Brown—not some Survey Monkey poll.

The best marketers know this—they know great work is what will save their jobs and enhance their careers. Five of them should be at the top of your prospect list. So how do you communicate with them? Creatively. Personally. Intimately. Intelligently. Professionally. Politely. What keeps most biz dev folks from doing this well is the fact they are also trying to communicate with hundreds of other prospects. If you were looking to get married, would you court 200 women? That's what this is—a marriage. It's not a "sales cycle." It's a courtship.

CREATING A CONTACT PLAN

A contact plan is a schedule. It reminds you when it is the appropriate timing for your outreach effort. I still don't know a better way to engage with the prospect than a compelling, insightful, and professional business letter. You can follow the hard copy letter with emails. The letter should ask for permission to engage. It acknowledges that you know they have an existing agency relationship that you respect, but also communicates a tangible benefit to the prospect for a continued dialogue. It should allow the prospect to opt out if he wishes. You'll be surprised how few will if you can inspire or educate. I've found that most marketers are passionate about what they do and like talking about it as long as you respect their time.

But, we know better. It doesn't always work that way. You may have to do something creative to catch your prospect's attention, an icebreaker. Ironically, this is what we claim we do for our clients—do something creative to get them noticed, build their brand, drive sales, yada yada. Yet it's now considered "too traditional" for us to do that for ourselves. Beyond the basic tools (a blog, a website, a book, a reel, an agency video—updated regularly)—we are further required to create an outreach "campaign" that will stand out, win its own awards for self-promotion, create a buzz and genuine interest from your prospect. Don't tell them you're creative—be creative. Is it worth it? Only if it's done right. This requires you to really be creative and not just say you're a creative agency. It requires you to hit a home run for your own team.

Let's be specific and look at a great creative "icebreaker outreach" campaign.

CASE STUDY: HAMMERHEAD ADVERTISING

Situation: A four-person creative agency in Hoboken, New Jersey. The two partners were creatives. Our strategy was to be the agency where you can do great work *and* not have to cross the Hudson. The prospects were all in New Jersey. We picked a few that needed better work and began sending them stuff. The problem we encountered was that most of the New Jersey companies are monolithic and nobody answers the phone. I spent half my day getting prompted to the company directory. So we needed a creative breakthrough to get our top prospects to take our call.

Creative Idea/Solution: A voicemail message campaign that parodied the "cold calling" process. You know those voicemail messages you get from politicians around Election Day? Yep. A series of five messages, staggered three days apart and funny as shit.

Result: A minimum of 2,000 daily website hits for nearly a month. Several prospects called us wondering when the next spot would run. We had requests for meetings, proposals and information. Not only did Garfield review the campaign and rate it 3.5 stars upon release, but also in his year-end advertising review, he voted the campaign one of the best 10 advertising campaigns *in the world* (not just self-promotion—*all advertising campaigns*). Most importantly, it separated us from "the pack" of cold callers to our prospects. We were able to kickstart our contact plan and begin a professional outreach program.

CASE STUDY: FIREHOUSE

Situation: We got wind that Haggar and Crispin had recently split. The much-ballyhooed "equity stake relationship" apparently fizzled. As a Dallas-based creative agency, we viewed Haggar as a terrific top prospect. They were a national account, based locally. And they already proved to place a premium on great creative. And heck, they didn't even have to give us equity in their company — just an initial project where we could prove our chops. Except I couldn't get their CMO to return my emails after a scintillating initial conversation (I finally got him on the phone at 6:45 pm one night) when he agreed to a lunch meeting.

Creative Idea/Solution: Since I had told him we were a creative shop — we decided to do a viral video idea to show him what we could do for Haggar (some viral spots for YouTube). We didn't shoot the Haggar spots (we didn't know enough about what he wanted at that point). Instead, we shot a pilot to a series of agency vignettes. The pilot featured the Firehouse President sitting at his desk — very deadpan, his natural demeanor — speaking agency speak; how his agency would like to help Haggar do some really cool stuff that got noticed by the target—guys like him, thirty-and-forty-somethings. After a minute of this he announces that if they can't have Haggar, the agency won't have any pants at all. The big reveal is, you guessed it, he stands up and he's got nothing but some tacky boxers on. For the next five days, we shot vignettes — security camera-type stuff—the agency at work. Everyone in their underpants. Yes, chicks too. Like the Hammerhead spots in the previous case study, the brilliance is not in the context, but in the delivery and content. Each vignette ended with a log-in to an agency Haggar microsite. Each vignette was sent via email to the prospect with body text claiming we would not put our pants back on until our prospect took a meeting.

Result: On Day 5, I got this email from the prospect.

PUT SOME PANTS ON FOR GOD'S SAKE!!
Michael, thanks for the ongoing entertainment.
We loved your vignettes and want to meet you.
Our Director of Consumer Marketing will reach out with details.

And then a week later, this email arrived.

Hi Michael,
Stephen asked that I reach out to you to schedule some time to better understand your capabilities. I am responsible for consumer marketing for both our men's and women's business. I could meet on Tuesday of next week at 3 p.m. or Thursday morning. We can

set something up here or we can come there. Let me know what works for you.

34

CASE STUDY:

BREAKING THE ICE WITH A TOP

PROSPECT BY SHOWING YOUR ASS

It can be frustrating—putting all this time into your business development program: creating a new business culture, assembling a council, doing your homework, getting smart on category trends, identifying your prospects...and then you can't even get your prospect to notice you. Well, why should he? You've done nothing for him—everything you've done up to this point has been for you and your agency. To expect him to drop everything and take your call is presumptuous, at best. If you're going to bother someone on a consistent basis—you'd better do more than talk about your agency. You'd better at least entertain your target.

As Gossage said, people filter their messages by what entertains them. *It doesn't matter what kind of transformation or revolution is occurring in our industry; once our messaging fails to entertain—our services are devalued* (entertainment includes "discovery"). So, therefore our initial outreach efforts to top prospects should reflect the kind of work we would do for them. It should have the same tone—speak their enthusiasts' vernacular. In short, it should reflect their brand. It should feature a skill that you can immediately bring to their existing marketing mix—in essence, giving them a taste of what you can do for them.

In the Hammerhead Case Study, it was obvious that our guys had a gift for radio scripts. For a New Jersey-based retailer, like Jackson Hewitt, that was pretty attractive. Especially when the radio they were getting from their agency sucked. It paved the road for an "idea" for a radio campaign come tax time.

I've found that most business development folks are pretty adept at talking about their agency and what it offers. However, the best ones lead conversations about the prospect's business. They rarely refer to their agency—and when they do, it's framed in a current or previous client's relevance to the prospect's business. Leave the credentials stuff to digital outreach. Attach a credentials link to an email following a real conversation. Don't always be closing. This is not *Glengarry Glen Ross*. You're not selling land investments.

Think of icebreakers in terms of a campaign. Stagger your messages. The first one will be ignored. Everyone sends out one cute thingy. By the last one, they should want more. It should be that entertaining. If you can't create an entertaining campaign for the prospect featuring the benefit of your agency's skills—then how can you expect the prospect to believe you can do it for their business?

A brief word on "viral" videos. The beauty of them is they are so easy and cheap to produce. All you need is a great idea. Creatives love doing them, even more than their client work. Clients love seeing them on YouTube. So do prospects. I recently had a prospect show me one in a meeting—unprompted. He just said, "Check this out—some guy in California sent me this." It was great.

If you're not doing them for your prospects—others are. And if you are, someone did one better than yours.

35

APPROACHING THEM INTELLIGENTLY: AN IDEA OR INSIGHT THAT WILL HELP THEM DRIVE BUSINESS

The first decade of the 21st century brought us two major recessions—the double whammy. It's fair to call this the *Recessionary Era of Advertising*. Under such circumstances, it's not difficult to understand why new business has become such a high priority for ad agencies.

In ten years, the function of agency business development has gone from a luxury to a necessity. In the 1990s, it was mostly larger agencies that could afford this "luxury" (a luxury employee is one who is not billable). Today, you can't afford *not* to have a dedicated new business program/function/person.

I talk to marketing directors every day. They tell me that they have never seen or heard more outreach by ad agencies than now. They receive countless tweets, calls, emails, materials, books, brochures, PDFs and live links. They tell me that

99 percent of the outreach is about the agency, their people, their awards, their case studies, their positioning, their cool office space, their latest hot campaign and their omniscience to all things pertinent to their business. What most agencies fail to do is demonstrate that they've given any thought to the prospect and their business challenges.

There's a myth floating out there that "all agencies look and sound the same" in their positioning. This claim was more accurate ten years ago. Since then, I've noticed that the better creative agencies do a great job of differentiating themselves. The top creative agencies recognized this and changed the way they communicated their offering and positioned themselves. It's funny how the best agencies did little communicating at all—they preferred to let their work speak for them. They showcased it on a neat site with as little of the usual salesmanship as possible. Their work was VISIBLE. People saw it and liked it. They talked about it. It won awards. Marketing directors noticed. Consultants noticed. They got invited to pitch and they won a few and lost a few.

Then the second recession hit and cash became about as tight as an old man returning soup to the deli.

Existing clients cut spending. New business reviews, while seemingly abundant, were more often than not futile fishing expeditions on behalf of struggling, unprofitable marketers. That's when everyone either became a new business director or hired one.

So that's the world marketing directors live in. They become boys in the bubble because everyone's a salesman selling their agency. There's a new way to sell. Our new business targets are smarter and hipper than ever. They're certainly younger than ever. They have more digital acumen than ever. But, do *not* let the presence of additional outreach tools like Twitter be a substitute for developing a personal relationship with your top five prospects. Do not let social media make you less social, or even anti-social.

The best way to differentiate yourself from other agencies and their outreach programs is to treat your top five prospects as clients. Up to this point we have:

- Gotten smart on their business
- Established credibility as a thought leader
- Been creative and entertaining
- Developed a relationship

None of those things has brought one dime into your agency from your top prospects. What they have done, however, is pave the road for you to do what you do best—help solve one of their critical marketing challenges. By now, you should have identified a gaping hole in the prospect's marketing mix that you can fill. You may even have an unexpected insight into their target or an opportunity they are missing out on in the marketplace. You have an idea that can help them drive business. If you don't by now, why are they even on your prospect list? Tell them you have an idea. They need ideas.

I've heard that Jack Connors was a master pitchman. Supposedly, he would always say in a meeting, "we've done some homework on your business, here are three things we think you could do right now." They weren't spec ads or media plans—but business ideas. The "idea" you bring to the prospect should never be ADVERTISING or creative. Make them pay for that. Besides, it's too expected—creative agency brings in fluff, free, spec creative. They will not value a free product. Creative work is your product. You will surprise them with a business idea or a target insight. You don't need to blow it out. You don't need fancy boards or PowerPoint.

Tell the prospect you want to meet for twenty minutes at the mom-and-pop coffee shop closest to their office. If you have to go to Starbucks, okay—but I find most of them too loud and *wired* (gee, imagine that). Show the prospect your idea on a napkin. Don't let them have the napkin. Get clarification on the potential for them to execute your idea. Explore other opportunities in their mix. Find out who else would be involved in making a decision. Close on a meeting back at their office or invite them back to yours. If they agree, then you can blow the idea out and sell it in. You've hit a double off the wall. If not, your idea has warning track power.

Keep swinging for the fences. Maintain the relationship. Be professional. Your respectful persistence will be rewarded. Maintain an unwavering faith in your ideas. Your ideas will become meetings. Your meetings will become projects. Your projects will become retainers.

36

THE LEADS, THE LEADS, THE LEADS:
FINDING AND QUALIFYING LEADS
FOR YOUR CREATIVE AGENCY

David Mamet may very well be the voice of our generation, perhaps the most riveting social commentator of the past thirty-five years. Playwrights inherit a unique responsibility to the masses. It is incumbent upon the playwright to hold a mirror up to society and reveal to us for the first time who we really are. They accomplish this by delivering insights into ourselves that we cannot see without their plot and character development. They also inherit the kindred spirit of the Bard of Avon, who held up said mirror better than anyone.

Mamet writes dialogue ("Mamet speak") in the same familiar manner that we speak today—just as Hemingway wrote in the vernacular of his time, eighty-some-odd years ago (strangely Papa's novels now read the same way an early Springsteen record sounds—embarrassingly dated). Reading Mamet's works can only help us write more effectively for today's intense staccato marketplace, and therefore, communicate better to it. Seeing his films can only increase our creativity. But, experiencing one of his plays as a live performance can *transform* us. To study a Mamet script is a journey into the art of communicating—his tales totally rely upon minimalist but colorful language and dialogue. I confess, I find it mildly interesting that Mamet, Hemingway and Springsteen all sported beards (and for that matter, Shakespeare, too).

Glengarry Glen Ross, perhaps Mamet's best-known work, is particularly relevant to agency new business. The action is primarily centered upon "leads," ultimately the Glengarry leads. New business professionals must accept that they are first in the lead generation business. As much as we are now grounded in a search engine-based marketplace, we cannot simply blog and tweet, then sit and wait for an email response to our latest newsletter. We can't just track the daily click-throughs to our website. Social media doesn't replace the need to generate and act upon leads. It augments it. It's another road, not the only road. At some point, we must make a sales call and ask for the meeting—or send a sales email requesting the same.

Everyone's favorite scene in *Glengarry Glen Ross* seems to be the seven-minute "motivational" speech Alec Baldwin delivers to the boiler room of a real estate telephone sales team (whose members include some of the finest actors of the era—Al Pacino, Jack Lemmon, Alan Arkin, Kevin Spacey and Ed Harris—none of whom wore beards, except Pacino in *Serpico*). It's a tour-de-force performance, with several lines forging their way into the lexicon of the contemporary sales and marketing person:

"Coffee's for closers."
"Always be closing."
"Get them to sign on the line which (sic) is dotted."
"The leads are weak? You're weak!"

37

THE LEADS:
FOLLOW THE MONEY

Identifying and tracking a lead is like trying to find out the real truth about anything—start by following the money. Does it surprise anyone that one of our planet's largest depositories of gold and precious metals was housed in the basement vaults beneath the World Trade Center? Should we be surprised that certain politicians (vice presidents, for instance) profit lavishly from war? Or that insurance company CEOs had a very good decade? Stop me now before Omnicom begins monitoring my content.

You can call me a conspiracy theorist, but that's what they want you to think.

While there is a dearth of creativity in the world today, there is no dearth of financial news and reporting. Therein lies the gold mine of new business leads. *The Wall Street Journal* refuses to give away its content for free. Why? Because their stock-in-trade is valuable content/information that most of the business community cannot live without.

The business and financial wire services are rife with leads, almost hourly. The trickle down effect from the venerable *WSJ* to your local business rag is instructively correlative.

Most smaller creative agencies can't chase every NASDAQ bubble stock, but we can track our local business chronicle for cash infusions, venture capital, and newly budgeted product or service launches. I've found that many of these boons are often connected to a larger financial trend in that particular category or niche industry.

Go back to basics and study the national and local business journals. Focus on categories that best fit your experience. Keep a folder of financial bubbles and trends in your categories. It occurred to me that if everyone spent as much time on the business news wires online as they do on Facebook, maybe they wouldn't need to be tweeting for dollars or relying on social media to do their job for them. I've found that the majority of leads I've generated from social media ultimately became tire-kickers, or worse, underfunded marketers looking for an agency to magically feed the multitudes with fishes and loaves. Wouldn't you rather follow the money and try to control your fate than be at the mercy of Twitterdom? What appears to be the land of milk and honey may just be a mirage.

I like to hole up with *The Book of Lists* and a Cuban cigar and play bounty hunter. Every metropolitan market has a Book of Lists published by the local business journal. It may be the most underutilized tool in the new business community. For small agencies, try the *Financial Times'* "America's Fastest-Growing Companies" list. I also like the listings of VC firms. For another angle, look at the Best Places to Work. There is a good chance that companies, who are good to their employees, are probably good to their vendors and strategic/ creative alliances. Read the bios of the top executives, because what's at the top usually trickles down.

There are other services dedicated exclusively to lead generation for ad agencies—these are usually the product of someone else doing this very same homework for you. You could do the same thing for yourself if you weren't on Facebook telling all your "friends" how smart or cool you are. Or tweeting. Or blogging. Or wallowing in LinkedIn, the land of the unemployed and disenfranchised shill.

Most of these agency-focused lead services just comb the wires for press releases of announcements like new CMO hires. I've followed up on many of these so-called leads from pubs like Pearlfinders and The Delaney Report and usually the "lead" has been so bombarded by agency outreach that they have already retreated to their underground asylum. Think about it, you are paying to share leads with hundreds of agencies. I consider a new hire an okay lead. But, I'd rather follow the money; it almost always leads to the truth.

38

THE LEADS:
WHAT TO DO WITH A
QUALIFIED LEAD

Okay, you've hunkered down at your laptop on the business wires. You've paid particular attention to your niche industries. You've combed through *The Book of Lists* and separated the wheat from the chaff. You've subscribed to and tracked the trade pubs in your focus categories. This does NOT mean *Adweek*, *Ad Age* or the other advertising trade pubs. Instead, I am referring to *Restaurant News*, if you are focusing on the dining category or retailwire.com if you are chasing Big Boxes. And, finally, a tactic I am quite fond of, you have attended trade shows/conventions in your sweet spot industries (a great opportunity to canvas an entire category—like an all-star summer camp for a basketball recruiter). You evaluate, qualify and prioritize your list of leads—now what? This is usually the juncture where paralysis sets in.

Moving on a qualified lead is a lot like dating. There is an unwritten protocol, decorum. Here are six things to avoid in the dating/qualified prospect outreach process. (Let's have some fun with this).

1. *The Wichita Lineman.* Avoid repeated phone calls. There's a fine line between stalking a qualified lead and nurturing a potential relationship. Constant calling is a sure-fire way to get your calls screened out. Instead, deploy a holistic communications strategy: including emails, direct mail, hand-written notes and modest gifts. I like to send food, like sopressata, especially if it's an Italian guy—everyone likes free food, if it's good.

2. *He Ain't Heavy, He's My Brother.* Don't get too personal, especially with what you send out. I mean a little sopressata among *paisanos* is one thing, but bringing race, religion or politics into the mix (especially early in the sales cycle) is a no-no. Just because you read that your prospect is a member of the local Christian CEO Bible study, stay away from the John 3:16 stuff for now. And please, stay apolitical—there's enough of that everywhere you turn. Finally, whatever you do, keep race entirely out of it. In short, don't be smarmy. Instead, send your prospect tickets to a ballgame.

3. *I Don't Wanna Know (the reasons why).* No potential customer or partner wants to be viewed as a sales lead, quali-

fied or otherwise. Avoid technobabble like, "I noticed you opened our last email and clicked all the way through," or "Thanks for visiting our website recently." It just feels gooey. Instead, tell them your sister attended their alma mater. It doesn't matter if you don't have a sister, at least that's better than making the prospect feel like you've got them on the GooCam.

Buckingham Nicks was one of my favorite bands. It's not that they had a string of big hits. They didn't until they became Fleetwood Mac. But the relationship between Lindsey Buck-ingham and Stevie Nicks was touching. They loved and needed each other. They relied upon each other, in life and onstage. I liked their things better than John and Yoko's. It just felt more genuine to me. (Fleetwood Mac—"I Don't Want to Know")

4. *The Great Exaggerator*. Does anything turn off people faster than some blowhard inflating their statistics or case stud-ies? Or distorting sales numbers beyond belief ("same-store sales went up 52% and brand recall hit 111%"). In-stead, leave numerology out of the relationship entirely. It's just a number and it doesn't solve the prospect's prob-lem. Instead, give the credit to your client who trusted you with his business and acknowledge his courage.

Soul Asylum is a curious case for the ephemerality of the alter-native music machine. They went from cult icons to mainstream hitmakers in the 90s. And then, with the advent of the Internet as the primary server of pop, they vanished into the millennium; until they resurfaced in 2006 with a polished album of mature, adult rock n' roll (talk about a triple oxymoron). Well, I liked it anyway. (Soul Asylum—Great Exaggerator)

5. *Nowhere Man.* "...doesn't have a point of view/knows not where he's going to./Isn't he a bit like you and me?" How many salesmen try to hit on this prospect? Hundreds? Try thousands, annually. You are just drone. Sales babble. An uninvited guest. Or worse, a gatecrasher. So you have two minutes to cut through the clutter. Telling the prospect what he already knows won't cut it. Somehow, you need to make an impression. And you only have one chance to make a first impression. Be a personal brand. Have an informed, educated, and insightful opinion. Stand for something so when you call back, he'll think, "oh yeah, that's the guy who..."

6. *Burning Questions.* Every sales coach in the world preaches the power of the leading question...the closing question...the burning question. Is there anything more irritating than a salesman who calls you and asks a question ending with the word "correct?" You know, like "Mr. Palma, your investment portfolio is underperforming, correct?" I refuse to answer any question thats ends with "correct?"
    Throw the old book out. Stop being presumptuous and

borderline rude. It's early in the sales cycle. The most incendiary question is, doubtlessly, "What is your budget?" Think about it—you're like a guy on the street (except you're not even on the street, you're on the phone) and you stop someone and ask, "Hey, how much money do you have?" "Can I have some? I'll help you make more." Instead, keep your early questions big picture, like: "What's your vision short-term?"

Just for fun, five questions to avoid on a first date:

1. "Do you eat beef?" (ice water, menus)
2. "Do you believe in the single-bullet theory?" (first drink: Single Malt scotch on the rocks—an ill-advised play on the word "single")
3. "Are they real?" (wine, with dinner)
4. "Have you ever been to DUI school?" (more wine)
5. "I'm going to Havana, you wanna go? (black coffee, 10 p.m.)

Tips

FOR CREATIVE PROFESSIONALS

39

ON WRITERS, COPYWRITING, AND HOW TO BUILD A PORTFOLIO

The utter audacity to call yourself a writer! Now that takes *cojones*. Writers are born with an acute sensitivity to the human condition (in this way, they are "chosen") and then they are self-made through reading, studying and, well, *writing* (then, rewriting). You must "invent" yourself as a writer. To think that you can play with words enough to massage them into something interesting and entertaining (and in advertising, sell something at the same time) requires a certain insouciant naiveté. And at the same time, it requires a willful dedication to language and style as well as devout discipline to practice the craft daily.

Writers are a rare breed, like southpaw pitchers in baseball. I've placed more writers than any other type of talent—

hundreds and hundreds of them. I don't know why. Maybe because the good ones are so rare. I've noticed an alarming de-emphasis of writing in the advertising industry in the past decade. I'm not sure if that's a result of the declining literacy of today's audiences or the slow extinction of the breed providing less written content, or both. But, it's almost odd to see a "writer's campaign" today. Everything is so visually driven—hinging on a "concept" (usually shock value or a slapstick gag—like the Betty White spot).

I'm not just referring to the print medium. It's also TV, Radio (how can radio be so poorly written and dependent on clichéd sound-bite gags?), online, and outdoor (all you have to write is seven words). I'm also not necessarily referring to a lot of body copy or words.

Take Google's iconic Super Bowl spot. It was a delightful narrative; a coming of age story allegorical to all Google users (that would be everyone with an Internet connection). Not one spoken word, just three and four word "googles."

I'm also not referring to nostalgic Neil French/David Ogilvy exhaustive print tomes drawing upon Noel Coward drawing-room humor. More along the lines of the Avis' "The Other Car" television campaign. Brilliant. These days, a writer's campaign sticks out like a boner in a lesbian bar.

Pardon me while I digress on radio. It's not going away. People drive to and from work. Most of America does (check out the HOV lane). Yes, the dork in the Beamer has SiriusXM, but most of America listens to the radio. Every day. Even with Spotify and iPhones—radio remains a viable medium. I can't think of a better way for an advertising writer to prove they can write than to author an entertaining and sustainable radio campaign. Think Tom Bodett. The Folgers Coffee Couple. Molson.

I know for a fact that agencies discourage radio from their clients' media mix because they can't fulfill the creative. I once sent a young writer to interview with Lee Clow in Venice. He turned the job down and subsequently founded a successful radio scriptwriting agency. That's how rare the skill set is—they don't need Chiat/Day. As an aside, I listen to *1690 AM Atlanta WMLB "The Voice of the Arts."* Stream it into your agency, set it on your laptop at work. It is guaranteed to inspire you and increase your creativity.

I'm often asked by writers for assistance in constructing their portfolios. What's most striking about young writers' portfolios is the absence of evidence that they can actually write. I visited an esteemed portfolio school not too long ago and reviewed several dozen student's portfolios. *What are they teaching them there?* Certainly not how to write interesting or entertaining copy. I can't tell the difference between the copywriters and the art directors. I can't find the headline. There isn't any headline. The body copy, if there is any, reads as if it were written by Jeff Spicoli. No radio scripts to be found anywhere.

Here are some tips to help guide you in building a writer's portfolio:

1. *Provide examples that you can actually write.* Show us you can do more than just think visually in advertising terms. Show that you are actually a writer, as you purport to be. Headlines that inspire, compelling body copy, radio scripts and TV scripts with dialogue. You get it.

2. *Provide examples that you can sell something.* I ran a search for an Executive Creative Director at one of the Southeast's largest and best-known agencies. We reviewed a dozen or so candidates' portfolios. There was a lot of humor (really funny shit), pathos (Goosebump City, near Rineytown) and whacked-out weirdness (half the stuff we saw we didn't understand until the third or fourth view). But there was very little selling happening. I am not just referring to price/item dreck retail formulas, but basic brand/product/benefit advertising that is interesting and entertaining. Sell me something, dammit.

3. *If it's not great, there's no place for it.* This especially applies to TV. One of the hazards of personal websites is the temptation to over-indulge in your own work. Treat it the same as an actual hard case portfolio. It only takes one mediocre campaign to get someone to click away from your site.

4. *Be interesting, but not too cute.* Tell us a bit about you *without* actually telling us. Hell, you're a writer. Figure out a way to make yourself entertaining without trying too hard. Use music, film, theatrics or something topical to augment your work. Don't overdo it, but using a snippet from an obscure Monkees tune as intro music is a nice touch.

5. *Yes, show digital, duh.* Everyone shows basic websites, banners, and promos they've created. Very few show them in nontraditional ways through cool applications, videos, games and original content written for websites (beyond basic yada "Who We Are" stuff). Live links are okay, but remember they take people AWAY from your site.

6. *Order your work so it tells a story.* Make it a "book within the book." Make it a narrative. Leave 'em laughing or crying.

7. *Stay away from spec unless you have nothing else.* Sell an ad.

8. *Be a headline machine.* If someone puts fifty cents in, give them a case of headlines. There will always be a place in this business for a headline machine.

9. *Radio.* This can be spec if you have none produced. You can produce your own on basic Mac apps like GarageBand. I'm waiting for the young writer to produce a radio campaign for himself—just to show me he can do it.

10. *Keep the gimmicks to a minimum.* Be interesting and entertaining, but not weird. We all know you're weird—you're a writer. Don't rub our nose in it.

I'll close with some of the infamous CP+B Copy Test. Devised by a writer I placed there about twenty-five years ago—Bill Wright, employee number 28. Bill is now the Creative Director on Burger King. He noticed some of the same disconcerting trends in young writers that I mentioned above. So he implemented a copy test as part of the hiring regimen at Crispin.

THE CP+B COPY TEST

- Give a short, persuasive argument on letting Pluto remain a planet.

- Pen a haiku about prairie dogs.

- Describe toast to a Martian in fifty words or less.

- Describe the color red to a blind person.

- "Employees must wash their hands before returning to work" is such a boring sign. Its ubiquity has rendered it useless (a sobering thought). For all humanity, please rewrite it.

- You might be redneck if:

- Write a really awful pun.

- Match the airline with its hub airport.

- What's your favorite oxymoron?

- What's your favorite retronym?

- Write twelve synonyms for the word "Go."

- Now write twelve antonyms for the same word.

- Extra credit: Diagram the Preamble to the U.S. Constitution.

40

ON WRITERS,
THE ELEMENTS OF STYLE

Yes, writers are a peculiar and dwindling lot. Without writers, what would we read? Lately, I've taken to buying and reading books on my iPad. I just finished T.J. English's, *Havana Nocturne: How the Mob Owned Cuba and Then Lost It To the Revolution.* I'm now beginning Jane Leavy's *The Last Boy: Mickey Mantle and The End of America's Childhood.* Neither book is terrifically well-written, nor riveting. The subjects are interesting and occasionally fascinating, but the prose itself lacks a certain craft—a style. This reminded me that we are not to confuse topical or entertaining content with good writing.

As W.H. Auden said so well, *"It is the duty of the writer to make language new."* I know, I beat that line into the ground, but it's the best one I've ever heard about writing. I didn't understand this at first. Or, I understood it on an academically superficial level. But, when I first read Jay McInerny's *Bright Lights, Big City* in the mid 1980s, I finally grasped what Auden meant.

It reminded me of Kerouac, in that each page was exciting—not so much for the narrative—but for the language and the style. When a great narrative meets original style, you have a masterpiece, like *The Great Gatsby*. It doesn't have to be a novel. It can be an essay like Updike's "Hub Fans Bid Kid Adieu" or journalism. Actually, one of the most compelling works I've ever read is *Industrial Society and Its Future* (a.k.a. *The Unabomber Manifesto)*. Revolutionaries make great writers—I regularly read Fidel Castro's weekly column, *Reflections*.

Strunk & White have taken a lot of hits. Long dismissed by the high-waisted, khaki-wearing academic set as "50 Years of Stupid Grammar Advice"—yet, just the title itself, *The Elements of Style*, strikes a chord in me. It begs the question, "What makes a writer a good writer?" I keep going back to Auden's quote, but that too lacks instructiveness. Sure, Dylan can write songs, but what makes them good lyrically? What makes Howard Gossage special? What makes an Updike novel an Updike novel? Well, it's the same thing that made Twiggy a sensation, and Jackie O an institution: STYLE.

How does one define style, then? That's a bit like trying to catch lightning in a bottle (eek, what a cliché!). That's like trying to describe the color red to a blind person (there you go! make language new). Or diagramming a play for Julius Erving. Style repels definition. It relies on grace, color detail, and description. These are some of the elements of style, but they are not style itself. Style is distinctively original and inimitable, yet entire industries thrive by mimicking it. You can write like Bob Dylan, but you can never be Bob Dylan.

Narcissistic writers reveal themselves. Their verbosity overwhelms the narrative, the lyric or the ad. Don't confuse description with verbosity. Even if you are a walking thesaurus, you are still not a gifted, stylish writer. You just have a good memory. That will get you through college, but it won't win you the Pulitzer Prize—or even a One Show Pencil.

Style derives from acumen and attention to detail. It is learned in diners and train stations. It is acquired through experience by reading, listening and observing. Writing style begins with a sensitivity to the human spirit and condition. Writers look at the world differently. They extract meaning from the mundane. They distill amazement from the minutiae. This is why they are often monikered as "eclectic," as if they don't fit into society.

To illustrate the point of verbosity versus description, let's take a quick look at Bruce Springsteen's writing. His first three albums are verbose beyond immediate assimilation. Clearly, a young, ambitious (and somewhat narcissistic) writer trying really hard (maybe too hard) to be a poet. I like some of those songs, they're good. But with his next three albums, he grew as a poet and did what all great writers learn to do: SAY MORE WITH LESS. He became a reductionist. He made language new. *Darkness On the Edge of Town, The River,* and *Nebraska,* with their minimalist, austere and stripped-down lyrics are works of a disciplined writer. I'm not knocking the first three records, but it's instructive to see how the writer evolved from an ebullient romantic to a disciplined realist. In short, writing is not typing. It's typing, editing, and reducing.

What does all this have to do with advertising? I read a lot of "agency positioning" stuff.

Everyone seems to have a new tagline for their agency: "Rethink Everything," "The Factory," "Brand Storytellers," and "Ideas for the New Whatever." Yada yada. My favorite agency tagline is eighty-four years old, McCann-Erickson's "Truth Well Told." This captures my point in three words more accurately than this entire chapter (talk about verbosity!). It's not the content, or the concept, for that matter, that is king. It's the *way* agencies tell the story that brings value to brands and clients. Yes, we need a good story, just like Updike needs a good narrative. But, what makes Updike Updike is the way he tells his story. Many great ad concepts died from failure to tell the story compellingly.

I hear so much stuff from or about writers these days—"digital writer," "heavy broadcast writer," "conceptual writer," etc. How about just being a WRITER? Write something I want to read—something that entertains, educates, motivates, inspires, gives me goosebumps, or makes me laugh or cry. If you can do that, you are a writer.

41

MAKING IT IN TODAY'S BRAVE, NEW CREATIVE WORLD

So, where is the writer's place in today's marketplace? How does one make a decent living these days spinning words? Advertising copywriters are at the top of the financial food chain. Journalists and academicians are paid paltry wages in comparison. Trade writers are the bottom feeders. Yet, there is a fine line between the skill sets of trade scribes and ad copywriters, and the line is getting grayer. So how does today's writer distinguish him or herself from a lowly tradie or newspaperman?

Well, to get to these answers we should first look at how copywriting has changed. In the thirty-five years that I've recruited writers, I've noticed a gradual erosion of the craft (that's not new news). But, that erosion is more likely the result of adaptation than decay. Media has changed. EVERY-

THING is media, therefore I guess everything has changed. But mostly, writing itself has changed because READING has changed. The craft adapted to the practice. I went to a Barnes & Noble recently. I depressingly felt like I was in the new Blockbuster Video retail environment. I couldn't escape two striking observations:

- Coffee table books ruled. And they were mostly heavily discounted.
- *Books for Dummies* have grown out of control, like some literary form of kudzu.

What does this mean (other than the fact that I felt perfectly comfortable in a literary environment targeted to Dummies)? Well, you can take some liberties here and make your own connection. But, I'm guessing it's got a lot to do with the fact that increasingly more "real" books are purchased on iPads and Kindles. The rest of us morons go to Barnes & Noble.

"Real" reading is a largely digital experience today. Okay, how does that affect a person with a copywriting career? Professional copywriting has always rewarded versatility. We assume the pro can crank out headlines. Those are table stakes. A pro masters body copy that sells (sure thing) by making it interesting. Penning the seven-word billboard joke—they're comedians. And only now, have we crossed the Mendoza line.

The real hitters today pound out compelling and alarming tweets. They write engaging and entertaining online content.

The new visual format is the 15 or 20-second online spot—it's like "TV Lite." They can write natural and human dialogue that works in a television script. Above and beyond all, they can conceive a campaign that amazes from a single, simple idea. That's a lot to ask, but that's why they make the big bucks. Those folks could have been nationally syndicated columnists if they chose journalism as their professional writing career, or dramatists. They are the George Wills and David Mamets of our industry.

What appears to be somewhat scarce in the new breed of digitally nurtured writers is strategic marketing thinking. I read a lot of new stuff. Some of it is advertising. Some of it is... well, I'm not quite sure. But what sticks out like a sore thumb is a strategically connected thought, well written—in any media or format. A business idea well told. An enlightenment creates a sense of wonder, however ephemeral. The ability to kick a snare drum in someone's brain.

So, it is the Big Idea that remains the Holy Grail for writers. Big Ideas are simple. Multi-lingual. Cross-cultural. Timeless, yet "new" (not always in a contemporary way, but always in a fresh way). They hold a mirror up to society, or a targeted segment of it, in a way that reveals an unexpected truth. It can't be too unfamiliar. Simple. Yet, not too simple. Specific, yet broadly interpreted. Open-ended.

Where are all the big ideas out there? Everyone loves talking about them—about how they are the only true value ad agencies can provide to brands? And about how they are what separates creative agencies from technology marketing firms. But where are they? So often you see work that contains a big idea, but it's half-baked. Or rather raw. Big Ideas need to be fully baked, like ziti with grandma's tiny meatballs. I haven't seen much great ziti lately. Help me out; where are the big ideas? What will this era be remembered for? The Apple Store? What are the definitive concept-driven campaigns over the past five years to current—in this country, America, not some third-world country without an FCC.

Who is this era's Mr. Clean? Is it The Most Interesting Man in the World? The Brawny Man? Or a Subservient Chicken (that would be you, Mr. Hotshot Writer)? Please excuse me while I seek recluse to tend to writing my Great American Book for Dummies: Life for Dummies. It's a Cautionary Tale-Coming of Age-Allegory-Epic-spanning-four generations of a Sicilian/American family confronting the moral battleground of good vs. evil. It also contains a recipe for great ziti.

42

TEN TIPS TO IMPROVE
MENTAL TOUGHNESS

So you work in a creative industry. You are neither a war-
rior nor an athlete. Yet, your ability to survive and advance
often hinges on adaptation and perseverance. They require
guts, moxie, vigor, fortitude, mettle, spunk, grit, pluck, har-
dihood, backbone and several other descriptive synonyms of
"mental toughness."

Woody Allen said, "Ninety percent of success is just showing up." If that's true, the other ten percent hinges on mental
toughness. Anyone can be mentally tough. Certain challenges require extreme mental toughness, while others simply
require that we stay out of our own way and perform. Let's
confront the former: the tough challenge, the big pitch and
the presentation where the account is on the line; or away
from business, in a competitive golf or tennis match.

These tips apply; use them at your own risk:

1. *Stay In the Present*. You're only as good as your last win and you're only as bad as your last loss. But what does NOW require? The future is a seductive temptress, but it distorts the task at hand. Now and what you are doing now supersedes all.

2. *Trust Your Talent*. It's all you really have. It transcends your relationships, money, power and tactics. You can only control one thing: your mind. If you don't believe in your talent, your skill and your ability to do something when it counts, then you should do something else.

3. *Don't Beat Yourself Up*. This tip is related to #1, but extends the thought. Learn to let things go (bad things especially). It's not life and death. It's not cancer survival. It's advertising, tennis, golf or whatever. Small failures should embolden you and make you more determined.

4. *Maintain Unwavering Faith*. Borrowing from *Good to Great*— reject cynicism. Think good thoughts. Visualize success in the moment. Accept the bad breaks, there are more bad breaks than good breaks. They don't "even out." You cannot fail if you do your best.

5. *Love the Process*. Be ritualistic. Have a routine. Stick to

it. Stop worrying about results. Love the process. Love to compete. Creativity is rumored to be the opposite of routine—it's a bad rumor. Accept victory and defeat with equal dignity.

6. *Be Yourself.* To be yourself, you have to know yourself. Get to know yourself better. The best way to do this is to put yourself in unfamiliar situations. Don't accept in victory what you would not accept in defeat. If you're going down, go down as the person/player you are. Don't try to be someone else—or what others want us to be.

7. *Overcome Fear of Failure.* Yes, fear is the mortal enemy of creativity (thanks Alex). It's actually the mortal enemy of everything. Most psychiatric disorders and dilemmas are grounded in FEAR. There are literally hundreds of phobias—they all begin with "fear of... " So how does one overcome fear? Let go of all the stuff you can't control (your opponents, public opinion, your relationships). Stop trying to control EVERYTHING ELSE and start controlling the one thing that you can control: YOUR MIND!

8. *Practice "Up."* Whenever possible, upgrade your competition in practice. This will elevate your level of play when it really counts. Hold your work up to higher standards. Get better every day. False confidence is nearly as dangerous as fear of failure.

9. *Be Patient*. Sometimes it's best not to force the action, let the challenge come to you. Never panic. Wait for your opponent to panic, then pounce.

10. *Find Someone Who Believes In You*. We all need a coach, a mentor and a partner in whom we trust with our goals and fears—a confessor, a counselor. Someone who can challenge us to be our best, pick us up when we are down, remind us not to sulk or whine or just say nothing and support us with quiet confidence. Find them, they will help make you mentally tougher.

43

WHO IS THE NEW CREATIVE PERSON?

Creativity is making a comeback. After "tech-ing" up the past few years, agencies are beginning to remember what they actually get paid to do: create communications. The axis is shifting back to content from context. And that's a good thing.

Last week, Google paid $23 million for Frommer's, a relatively stuffy travel site. True, Google can pull $23 million out of the petty cash drawer, not a significant financial investment. But, it's the gesture that is symbolic. They paid for content (however pedestrian). The world's technology king, with all its crawlers and spiders, is buying creative content.

Through the growing pains of tech-ing up these past few years, agencies have lost their creative luster. The new breed: creativus millennial doesn't regard advertising as the creative cauldron of tomorrow. They're creating new forms of communication and it's not about sales—it's about engagement, it's experiential. They would rather work in Silicon Valley than on Madison Avenue.

Shoot, are there even any agencies left on Madison Avenue?

I see signs of things coming back full circle, however. Fifteen years ago, you could go into a new business presentation and simply tell the client, "we're gonna make your brand cool." If you had the work to back that claim—both in your portfolio and for them in spec—you had a chance of winning the account. Then came the triple-whammy recessions (dotcom bust, 9/11, mortgage crisis: bang, bang, bang) and the bean counters took over. ROI and compliance ruled the road. If you told a client five years ago that you were "gonna make their brand cool," they called security to escort you out of the building.

Well, I'm glad to report that it's kinda cool to be cool again. Which, in itself, is kinda cool. Clients and therefore agencies are recognizing that the channels are cool, the technology is cool, the new toys/devices are cool. So, the content needs to be cool, too. But the rules of engagement have changed. We're not selling anymore. We're telling. We're conversing.

So, who's this new creative person today? Nobody asked me, but here are some thoughts:

- *Seeks of the Absolute Truth About Everything.* This trait is often referred to by agencies as "curiosity." Creativity requires a lot of curiosity, for sure. But curiosity should lead to a great deal more—it should lead to an insatiable hunger for the absolute truth. The great creative work and solutions require you to seek the absolute truth about Everything.

- *Has an Acute Sensitivity to the Human Condition.* You are engaging real people, not consumers. You're conversing with the man on the street. If you blow off panhandlers and mock the poor, you're not a creative person. Stop pretending you are. The triple-whammy recession fractured the national and global psyche. Just because you took your IPO money and bought a Dorkmobile (BMW) doesn't mean you can be shallow or condescending in your communications.

- *Makes Language New.* Here we go again with W.H. Auden quotes. Today's creative person takes the familiar and creates a new vernacular. They translate the anachronistic into the acronistic (acronyms abound!). They are the Kerouacs that write the new Beat Poetry. They blog to change the world (www.diehipster.com).

- *Holds a Mirror up to Mankind.* They are the Modern Shakespeares and Eugene O'Neills. They chronicle everyday life and make it seem fascinating. They make the humdrum drum. They show us ourselves for the very first time. They reveal our flaws in ways that allow us to forgive ourselves.

- *Shows You the World as You Dream It.* Only dreamers can do this. Anyone can learn (understand stuff). Some folks can speak well (talk about stuff). But the rare creative person dreams—they dream up stuff. They turn reality into a dream.

44

HOW TO ENGAGE
WITH A HEADHUNTER:
CREATIVE EDITION

Well, now that most of us have survived and are fully vaccinated, we can focus on the business of your career/vocation. 2020 was hard on many advertising careers. The deluge of candidate inquiries to our Hot Jobs posts on LinkedIn far exceeded any other year in my thirty-five-year career as a headhunter for creative agencies. As a result, I learned so many valuable lessons in the Year of the Pandemic.

If you follow your LinkedIn feed, you'll read a lot about "recruiter ghosting." I understand the desperation and frustration of talented folks whose careers are derailed by unforeseen forces. Recruiters don't want to be "ghosts" (unless it's Casper the Friendly Ghost). We want to help our clients, do right by candidates and make a little bit of dough.

So what are the best practices for engaging a headhunter?

Since you've all asked, here's my opinion:

- Don't assume we keep up with our LinkedIn message inbox. Use email.

- Do not text a recruiter. Better to call and leave a voicemail than text. Text is for friends, families and clients. The definition of "client" is "someone who pays you."

- Manage your expectations accordingly. Most good recruiters are straight-commission (even those who work on retainers). We're trying to make a living too. We want to do the right thing (I think everyone does), but our job is to serve our clients.

- Be memorable and humble (a tough balancing act). The best candidates have a humble swagger.

- Stick to the two-minute drill. All communication, written and verbal, should not exceed a two-minute format.

- Get a designer to do an infographic for your resume.

- Make a 30-second video commercial for yourself.

- Did I mention be memorable AND humble?

- Do your homework on the recruiter to whom you are reaching out. Nothing is more exasperating than candidates asking for basic information available on profiles and websites ("Where are you located?")

- Be positive and apolitical. Obviously don't whine about your predicament.

- Trust your talent.

- Be specific, not broad. Say, "I want this kind of job in these kinds of cities for that kind of money." Not, "I'm open to anything." Don't chase a job you don't want to do just because you need money.

45

THE FIVE KEY QUESTIONS
TO ASK ON A JOB INTERVIEW

CANDIDATES CAN CONTROL THEIR FATE
BY ASKING THESE FIVE KEY QUESTIONS

Ok, I'm fortunate to have learned a few things after setting up 5,000 interviews in my thirty-five years as an agency head-hunter.

For one, many employers don't know how to interview talented candidates. For another, HR sticks too closely to specs and job descriptions. And most importantly, candidates are so eager to talk about themselves that they often fail to ask the right questions.

What are the right questions?

1. What do you expect me to accomplish in this role?

2. What current obstacles are there in the way to accomplishing these things?

3. What are the next steps in the hiring process?

4. Is there anything else you or I need to know?

5. When can I start? (assuming you want the job, ask for it)

Ask the first two questions early in the interview. Ask question 3 about midway through the interview. Save the last two for your "close."

Make sure you take notes and write down the answers you get. You are now ready to respond intelligently to the employers' questions framed in their own language and expectations. Control the interview, don't let it control you.

46

THE ARC OF A
GREAT CAREER: FIVE STEPS

What is it that makes for a great career versus a merely efficient one?

Many people do their jobs well enough to survive many years. They manage to avert layoffs, furloughs, downsizing and restructuring. Somehow, they prosper. They adapt. They advance. Yet they never achieve their fullest potential. They never seem to be completely satisfied with their lot in their professional lives. They never reach their full promise.

Conversely, there are the big winners—the great ones, "the ones who never yawn or say a commonplace thing, but burn like fabulous yellow roman candles exploding like spiders across the stars and in the middle you see the blue centerlight pop and everybody goes 'Awww!'"—Jack Kerouac, *On the Road*

What separates the roman candles from the matchsticks?

This marks my thirty-fifth year recruiting top professionals in the advertising industry. I'm fortunate to have a significant sample size to make observations and draw theories upon what separates the wheat from the chaff. What I've noticed is the stars all share a similar arc in their careers. In fact, the "arc" is actually a career that comes full circle—the hero's journey.

Nobody asked me, but these are the five steps:

1. STUDENT We all begin as novices. We all start the same way, in the metaphorical mailroom. Our careers are narratives, coming-of-age stories: allegories. A literal AND a figurative journey unfolds. Call us Ishmael, and our industry the Great White Whale. I remember cutting out the daily advertising columns from the *Wall Street Journal* and pasting them into a binder. This began in 1990, and by 1997, I filled up six large binders of advertising industry content that I studied every weekend. I slept with the Red Book. This is the time we begin building our career skills.

2. JOB A speaker at a Mary Kay seminar once spouted, "JOB is just an acronym for 'Journey Of the Broke.'" This is true. If you approach what you do every day as a job, that's all it will ever be. You will never make a lot of money, you will always live beyond your means. And your career "cycle" will become increasingly vicious. But, we all start as entry levelers. Our first "big break" is simply landing a job. Rule #1: Never let your boss beat you to the office in the

morning. My first big break came as an assistant basketball coach at The College of the Holy Cross. It's where I learned how to recruit and where I also learned Rule #1 from the head coach. It was great advice from a work ethic standpoint. This is the point of the arc where we begin defining ourselves.

3. CAREER Ah, this is what happens when we get good at what we do—when people value our work and our particular skills. These are the chapters of the allegory where our professional lives take on a direction. A roadmap develops. We stay the course. Our goals are met. We gain clarity. We adjust. We reinvent ourselves. We change, morph, transform. This is the time in our lives when we hit our stride.

4. VOCATION I speak often of the "vocation-based" professional mindset. At its core, it's approaching what you do as if it were a higher calling—as if your career chose you and not vice versa. It's the WHY we are, not the WHAT. This is pretty heavy stuff, when you really think about it. But, when it happened to me, it was truly an epiphany and changed my life. Crazy to think that my work was part of a bigger picture, a grander scheme. Crazy to think God could work his ways through my work ministry. Crazy to want to give something back. Uh...not so crazy. What will you be remembered as? What will be your legacy? This is the true mark we make.

5. STUDENT Elliptically, it all comes full circle—we wind up where we started. I can't say it better than this guy:

We shall not cease from exploration/And the end of all our exploring Will be to arrive where we started
And know the place for the first time.
Through the unknown, remembered gate When the last of earth left to discover Is that which was the beginning...

— T.S. Eliot, "Four Quartets"

It amazes me how many folks on LinkedIn describe themselves as "experts" at what they do, especially at this final stage of their careers. I'm leery of experts. I want to be remembered as a student.

Epilogue

Like the deflated basketball on John Thompson's desk, this book is over.

Basketball is just a game, and such a silly game at that. If I had to do it all over again, I would have played golf, because if I hit as many wedges as I practiced jump shots, I'd be on the senior tour today. When you think about what is actually happening on the court—putting a ball through a cylinder—how silly and insignificant in the grand scheme of things.

And advertising? What a silly industry and career. If you consider selling people fried chicken and beer artistic, maybe you need to find a new way to express your creativity.

If you've learned anything from reading this book, it's *talent is luck*. Success is luck. Luck may be when preparation meets opportunity, but it's still luck.

The most important thing in life is courage.

Life throws some tough punches, but courage leads all comebacks. In 2022, my daughter's world changed when she was sixteen years old. A serious spinal injury left her paralyzed from the waist down. Yet, her unwavering spirit to regain independence has been a powerful lesson in strength. Witnessing her fight has become my source of inspiration. She is my idol, even more than my father.

Want to see true courage? Visit Shepherd Center in Atlanta. There, you'll find people battling to take a single step, a feat most of us take for granted. It's a humbling experience that puts life's challenges in perspective.

By observing people struggling to simply walk, your own swagger will become a lot more humble.

AFTERWORD

I first met Mike Palma a little more than a decade ago when our company, Tombras Group, was a regional agency and just starting to break through in our efforts to become a truly national player. As part of our efforts, we needed to develop relationships with the best recruiters and agency search consultants in the industry, so it was a big deal when Mike came to visit our agency in Knoxville, Tennessee. Meeting Mike was a memorable experience. We are in a storytelling industry, and it became clear during our introductory dinner that Mike was one of the best storytellers I'd ever been around. It's no wonder that he was so successful recruiting basketball players and now over 1,500 advertising executives.

Since Mike was a former basketball player and coach, we timed his initial visit to the agency to attend a game at our suite at the University of Tennessee against a Top 25 nationally ranked team. When we got to the arena Mike told me he had run into the famous head coach of the opposing team outside the hotel before the game. Mike knew this coach from his previous life in basketball. The coach was surprised and happy to see Mike and asked him what he was doing in Knoxville. Mike explained that he was in town to meet with a client and asked the coach how he was doing. The coach explained that his pre-gameday ritual of taking a quick nap at the hotel had been ruined by someone's dogs barking in the adjacent room.

Mike told him, "That's horrible! Who would let their dogs do that at a hotel like this?" At that exact moment, Mike's lovely wife, Cameron, walked out of the hotel with their two dogs. Mike winked at the coach, and he said great seeing you again and good luck in the game! Stories like that are not uncommon with Mike Palma.

Later that night Tennessee won in a surprising upset. (Coincidence?) One week later Tombras landed a talented executive that Mike recruited for us and several months later we won an important review Mike ran for The Coca-Cola Company. That win helped change the trajectory of our agency. Over the next few years, we won several key accounts under the Palma purview on our way to national prominence.

This book, *Walk with a Humble Swagger,* has stories even better than the one above. These stories translate Mike's lessons from the court to the business world in both entertaining and educational ways. You'll laugh while you learn.

As a student of our industry, I read everything I can about advertising. There's no doubt in my mind that Mike is the best writer in our game. His blog mikepalma.com is a must-read chronicle of the advertising business. It's my favorite read.

When I think of Mike, I'm often reminded of a lesson he shared with me once from his former Coach, the late Jim Valvano. Life is essentially about two things: accomplishments and relationships. Over the years I've had the pleasure of continuing to work with Mike and that has led to some of the most rewarding relationships and experiences I've gotten to enjoy in my professional career. For that I'm grateful.

DOOLEY TOMBRAS

PRESIDENT OF TOMBRAS GROUP
2024 AD AGE INDEPENDENT AGENCY OF THE YEAR

ABOUT THE AUTHOR

Michael Palma is the founder and CEO of The Palma Group, a leading recruiting and consulting firm exclusively serving the advertising industry. For over 35 years, the firm has specialized in executive search, business development consulting, and agency search for brand marketers.

Through enduring partnerships with hundreds of agencies and thousands of top-tier candidates, The Palma Group has facilitated over 1,500 successful placements since 1989, establishing its position as a preeminent headhunting firm in advertising.

Before embarking on his entrepreneurial journey, Palma honed his competitive edge as an assistant basketball coach at Holy Cross. His deep understanding of recruiting, cultivated both as a high school All-American and a coveted college recruit sought after by coaching legends like Rick Pitino, Dick Vitale, Jim Boeheim, John Thompson and Jim Valvano, proved instrumental in his transition to the business world.

Recognizing his innate talent for relationship building and closing deals, Palma leveraged his recruiting prowess to establish The Palma Group.

ACKNOWLEDGMENTS

I guess the best place to start this is to thank Ripples Media for their faith in the manuscript and their belief that I have anything of value to offer anyone. It was Jeff Hilimire's vision of Ripples that made this a good fit. Thanks to Andrew Vogel for his editing and Burtch Hunter for his incredible design.

Special thanks go to Becky Bumgardner for re-connecting me with Dick Vitale after fifty years. I'm so grateful to Coach Vitale for writing such an inspiring Foreword to this book.

Next up is Dooley Tombras for composing the crucial Afterword. It's rewarding that the busiest man I've known in the industry would take the time to write such a sincere passage.

I'd also like to thank the dear friends who contributed accolades to the front end and back cover of the book:

- Alex Bogusky
- Guy Bommarito
- Eric Kallman
- Curtis Zimmerman
- Linda Bruno
- Linda SanGiacomo
- David Angelo
- Steve Connelly
- David Baldwin
- Billy Donovan
- Matt Doherty
- Jim McCaffrey
- Jeff Ruland

And there are all the folks who supported my efforts throughout:

- My mom and dad and my sister Lisa—a strong family, they are my rock
- My children, Michael, Mary Elle, and Mercy Grace
- My loving wife, Cameron
- Thanks too to Christy, the mother of our two wonderful children

I have to call out my associates, the folks I've worked with:

- My partner, Ryan Farinella, the future of The Palma Group
- George Swisher, who I've worked with for almost twenty years
- The late Nancy Hall, who was an early collaborator
- Trustworthy and loyal research assistants: Courtenay Cronin Dutton, Teri Thompon Hagedorn, Elizabeth Stickley Scott and Amanda Battey

Thanks to the coaches I played for:

- Jack Johnston
- Denny McCann
- Jim Valvano
- Frank Morris
- Carl Tacy

Thanks to the coaches I coached with:

- George Blaney
- Eddie Reilly
- Jim Corrigan
- Jeff Yohn
- Rad Brown
- Leroy McDonald

All my teammates at Sacred Heart School, St. Agnes High School, Wake Forest University and Iona College.

And eternal love and thanks to all the players who put up with me as a coach at Bishop McGuinness High School and Holy Cross College.

The thousands of ad agency people who we recruited as candidates over the past thirty-five years.

The many Palma Group's ad agency clients. Thank you all.

www.ingramcontent.com/pod-product-compliance
Lightning Source LLC
Chambersburg PA
CBHW051259120626
46547CB00015B/2003